Value

for a

Young Woman

# Values Stories for a Young Woman

### Edited by
Marilyn O. Diehl and Marta O. Smith

WALNUT SPRINGS PRESS

Walnut Springs Press, LLC
110 South 800 West
Brigham City, Utah 84302
walnutspringspress.blogspot.com

ISBN: 978-1-59992-858-6

# Table of Contents

VIRTUE

FAITH

Faith is not to have a perfect knowledge of things;
therefore if ye have faith ye hope for things which
are not seen, which are true.

–Alma 32:21

# Attack of the Bees

I have always loved animals, especially horses. In fact, I actually enjoy cleaning out a barn. After I received my associate degree in animal science, I did an internship at a place that specialized in training horses for clients. When the owners were traveling to horse shows with clients' horses, I was left in charge of a lot of extremely valuable stock, with each animal worth between $25,000 and $500,000. While the owners were gone, I also cared for their children. The older teenagers helped me with the horses.

One day I was riding with McKenzie in the front pen when we heard a frantic call from her brother Keegan.

"McKenzie! Come quick!"

We immediately rode to the back pen, where we saw a horrifying sight. Somehow a hive of wild bees had been disturbed and were attacking a little bay horse. He was hooked up to the walker along with four other horses to cool off after their daily exercise.

I had no experience with something like this. Suddenly inspiration flooded my mind. I knew exactly what I needed to do.

"Keegan, hook up the hose," I yelled. "McKenzie, turn off the walker, then call the vet! Keegan, you and your cousin get the other horses in the barn out of the way!"

"I don't think we need to call the vet," McKenzie said after turning off the walker.

"Just do it," I replied.

I had jumped to the ground, grabbed the hose, and started spraying the little bay gelding with water. That is when I realized the bees couldn't fly when their wings were wet. Then I started brushing off the bees and pulling them out of his mane. They left little white things on him that I thought were probably stingers. The horse's whole body began to swell from the stings.

When the vet got there, he quickly gave the horse a shot to counteract the effects of the stings. The vet told me that my quick action had saved the gelding's life.

By Dawn Olsen, as told to Marilyn O. Diehl

# Faith Stills a Riot

It was my privilege after my graduation from the University of Utah in 1936 to secure a position as housemother at the New York State Training School for girls in Hudson, New York. This institution was the equivalent of a juvenile rehabilitation facility. Five hundred girls were enrolled, ranging in age from eleven to twenty-one. They had been sent there for various offenses, from petty thievery to prostitution. The girls lived in cottages with about twenty-five girls to each cottage.

Certain radical groups started a rebellion to promote their cause. The newspapers covered the rebellion with tall headlines. "All eyes open—here I come—Justice." Somehow, several of our girls obtained butcher knives, pokers, cleavers, and hatchets. And now who was to approach those rebellious girls and restore order?

The superintendent of the school called me into her office. "Are you afraid of death?" she asked me directly.

I answered that I was not.

"I am choosing you, Miss South, out of a group of one hundred officers, because you are the only one who believes in God. Those girls would kill me if I went in there. That is what those men have put into their hearts. It would not matter so much to me—I have attained my years. But we believe that with your faith, it can be settled peaceably without further harm to anyone."

I was instructed not to lock the girls in their rooms, which was what we usually did at night. I would be locked in the cottage alone with them for a period of forty-eight hours. Above all else, I was not to show any sign of fear before the girls.

So, armed with the greatest weapon in the world—faith in the living God—I was ushered into the presence of fifty emotionally aroused, antagonistic girls, who were still armed with weapons of riot, still challenging anyone to restore any semblance of order.

I shall never forget the look in their faces, or the sound of the click of the key behind me. I prayed my most earnest prayer, which was not very eloquent, but was as sincere as prayers come: *Lord, you have been in tougher spots than this, but I haven't, so will you please take over from here?*

The Lord took over in a way that amazes and amuses me to this day. Using my voice, we said to those girls, "Could you please teach me how to 'truck'?" This was the dance step of the day, with steps so intricate that it always fascinated me to watch. Not all people could do it artistically—such fast-stepping, timing, and energy.

With my slowness, low blood pressure, and watered-down energy, they could see it was actually a physical impossibility for me to "truck." I'd had about all I could do with the Charleston. But it put them in the position of being my teachers, a position they jostled for.

One could almost see them melt. Some of their muscles were still flexing for a fight, so one of the girls would loan her butcher knife to one of the others while she danced with me. The rest formed a suspicious circle around us. But I caught on, with the Lord's help, and I trucked so truckingly that the girls fought for turns to dance with me.

To keep them thoroughly diverted until they were all exhausted, I took them on, one at a time, and we danced until they could dance no longer. They were soon asleep and I had strength enough to tuck them safely into their beds. After they had slept and recovered their strength—I wore them out, mind you—they regarded me with a great deal of respect. The rebellion was over.

Whenever I recall the sweetness, the graciousness, the protection to me at that time, I am always overwhelmed with love. I learned that day how near the Lord is to us always, if we trust in Him. This testimony of His love and nearness to me is my most priceless possession.

By Ruth South Soderborg; adapted by Marilyn O. Diehl

# Say a Prayer — now!

My cousin Sarah and I were driving from Idaho to Utah to attend another cousin's wedding reception. Sarah's mom had let us take her pretty red Mustang convertible, which she had recently bought, and the trip was turning out to be really fun. We were having a great time!

It was really dark by the time we reached the Salt Lake Valley, and we had just driven through a large swarm of insects, many of which ended up stuck to our windshield.

All of a sudden rain started to pour, smearing the bugs on the windshield so that we could see nothing, not even the tail lights in front of us. The windshield wipers were not helping, either. We were in the farthest right lane, and there was a semi-truck on our left and a concrete wall on the other side. There was no place to pull off the road.

I was the driver and could not close my eyes to say a prayer, and I probably could not have focused long enough to say one anyway, so in a very frantic voice, I said, "Sarah, say a prayer! NOW!" She did. She asked that we would be safe and that we would be able to see the road in front of us.

Right after she said "Amen," the rain let up slightly so that we could make out the road in front of us, which was good because we were going around a curve. We took the next exit and found the closest Wal-Mart and were able to change our windshield wipers. I know that we were saved because we had faith. We made it to our aunt's house late that night and were able to attend the wedding reception the next day.

By Jasmine Latimer

# The Special Flour Barrel

In 1888, my family and I, along with several other families, moved to Afton, Wyoming. We lived in dugouts and were often deprived of provisions because of the condition of the roads, the weather, and the long distance to travel by team and wagon. Many times the women were left alone while the men and boys went for supplies, a distance of many miles. We gathered sego lilies, dandelions, and pig weeds for greens. Our other food was often rationed while we waited for supplies.

Many times the neighbors ran out of flour. There would be a knock on the door and someone would say, "Senie, can we borrow some flour? We're all out."

"Of course," I would reply. "Come in a minute while I get some."

We all shared with each other while waiting for supplies. Each time I went to get flour for my family or the neighbors, the barrel seemed to have just enough flour left for one batch of bread. This amount fed many and lasted until my husband pulled into the yard with supplies. On one occasion, shortly after he arrived but before he had filled the barrel, I went to the barrel to get flour to make gravy, and there was not even a tiny speck left. I always bore testimony that the Lord blessed me for being kind and helping those in need.

By Rose Scoresby, Ruth Haderlie, and Bertha Christensen;
adapted by Marilyn O. Diehl

# Falling

This all started at one of my favorite places in the whole world—girls camp, where girls have fun and strengthen their testimonies at the same time. I loved it there, and I want to go back every year I'm allowed. But nothing strengthened my testimony more than falling down a mountain. Well, I didn't really fall down a mountain. It was more like falling down while skidding on my knee on a steep trail descending from a mountain. I'll start at the beginning.

I woke up in the morning with a start when my best friend Kenna shook me. "Bailee, the buzzer thing went off, and now we have five minutes!" "Wow!" I screeched as I leapt out of my sleeping bag and tripping over Quinci, my sister, I pulled on a shirt and some random pants I saw lying on the floor. I was putting on my lanyard when Autumn, one of my friends, said, "We need to wear our girls camp shirts for the hike today." I frowned at her. "What? Do we have to?" I dove back into the tent and put on the girls camp shirt over the one I was already wearing. "Thanks," I shouted to Autumn as she walked away with Quinci to the devotional. I slipped on my CamelBak water pack and ran to catch up.

We sat on the benches facing the stage and sang along with all the songs with the YCLs (young camp leaders). Then we packed up to go on the five-mile hike. I hopped in the closest empty car, Sister Posposil's, and off we went. I listened to people's conversations as we traveled the winding road up the mountain. Finally, we reached our destination, the trailhead for the hike. "Okay, girls, stand in a line for head count," a leader said. I was standing between Kenna and another friend, Hanna.

Soon, we marched into the forest. After a while, my feet started to hurt. We walked farther and my back was killing me. I drank a lot of water, but it only helped my pain a little. When we finally stopped to rest, I leaned on a tree and slumped over. The leaders talked about the clouds and which kind is which. I sat there listening for a good ten minutes. Then we started walking again. "Don't worry, the rest of the way is downhill," said a YCL. She was totally wrong at that point, because we were climbing uphill for the next hour! "Hey, your descending's ascending!" shouted one of the YCL's fathers, a chaperone on the trip.

This is where it went downhill, but only for me. I suddenly got really dizzy. I told Sister Packard, and she told me to drink more water. Half an hour later, my dizziness got even worse. I was dragging my feet. We were finally going downhill. I felt my forehead, and it was cold. I had trouble breathing. *What is happening to me?* I wondered. Then I remembered something—something so important it never left my mind after I learned it. In my head, I listed my symptoms: dizziness, shortness of breath, cold skin.

Oh, no! I knew what was wrong with me—heat exhaustion. I hate that I knew that, right then and there, because I tripped, then skidded on my knee down the trail for about five feet. Pain erupted from my knee. I cried out in agony.

Sister Packard and my friends came over and tried to help me up. I cried out and dropped to the ground once more. I grabbed my knee. I couldn't bend my leg. I closed my eyes and prayed as hard as I have ever done in my entire life. Then everything went silent.

Time seemed to slow down. I heard a voice—a sweet, calm voice—say, "Do not be afraid. Everything will be all right." I knew that voice. I'd heard it before, but where? I opened my eyes, and my pain was gone. I looked at my knee. I tried to bend it, and it was fine! I was so happy, I was crying. Then I remembered the voice.

"Bailee, are you okay?" asked Kenna as she bent over and helped me up. "Did you hear . . .?" I said. "Hear you scream? Yes, and I was worried!" Sister Packard said. "No, did you hear a man?" I asked. They all looked at me like I was on drugs or something. "The only man here is the chaperone," Autumn said. It was weird how they dismissed the subject like that.

I walked one step and felt a tiny pinch of pain, but that's it. "I'll be okay, but it looks like I'm out of water. Did you bring an extra water bottle?" I said to Sister Packard. She handed me one and we descended the mountain.

When I fell, I thought I would die of the pain. But then the Spirit spoke to me, and the Lord immediately helped my knee to get better. He carried me that day, and I will never forget the feeling of love I received that day from Him and my friends. I will treasure this experience forever.

By Bailee Eaton

# The Power of Prayer

It was 1929, and people didn't explain things like a miscarriage to an eight-year-old like they do now. I knew bad things were happening, but what did it all mean? My parents left and my mother's parents arrived. Soon my aunts and uncles started showing up. My older sister and brothers were all there.

Then my father called from the hospital to talk to Grandpa. My mother was very ill, and Dad told him, "The situation is desperate. The doctors aren't sure they can save her."

Mother received a priesthood blessing, and we all gathered together in a prayer circle to fervently plead with Heavenly Father to save her life. When I was older, my mother told me, "The doctors were frantically working to try to stop the bleeding, and I was in terrible pain. I was suddenly above my bed looking down at those who were trying to save me. Then I found myself in a peaceful place surrounded with beautiful flowers. Your grandfather [my father's father, who died thirteen years earlier] appeared to me. He didn't actually speak, but he communicated to me that I had a choice.

"'If you choose to do so, you may stay here out of all the pain, or you can go back to earth and finish raising your family,' he told me."

Mother chose to raise her family and eventually had two more children. A skilled doctor was able to correct her physical problems, and she regained her health after a few months.

This experience left me with a lifelong trust in the power of sincere prayer. It had a great influence on me, especially when I was making the most important decisions in my life.

By Beth R. Olsen

# Faith Epiphany

"Are you crying?"

I quickly wiped my face. I hadn't heard my husband come in the front door. All my attention had been on the computer screen as I wrote a dramatic scene in my manuscript. I could still feel my heart beating just a touch harder than when I sat down to write at my dining room table earlier in the evening.

"Are you okay? Did something happen to one of the boys?"

I looked up into my husband's worried blue eyes and smiled. "Everyone is fine, Mike."

I watched him study my face for a moment before his stare fell to my computer. He slid his police radio out of its holster and placed it on the table, then removed the duty belt from his waist. "Was it something you read?"

"No, it was something I wrote." I got up and walked around the table, straight into his open arms. "I had an epiphany."

"Sounds painful," he joked. Then he asked seriously, "Is that what the tears were for?"

"It's silly, really, but I had what some writers call an 'aha' moment while writing the dialogue for this scene I've been avoiding."

"And that made you cry," Mike said, holding me closer.

"It . . ." I pushed out of his arms and sat down in the window seat, struggling for the right words. "In my story, Clair's mother had cancer, and she's trying to tell the guy she's falling in love with how she had prayed since she was a small child for her mother's miracle cure—"

"Like you told me you did for your mother." Mike sat down next to me and slid his fingers though mine.

I nodded. "And like my mother, Clair's mother died. But writing the dialogue between the two characters, it was like I was having this surreal conversation with myself, except one part of me was this bratty child arguing that I didn't get my prayers answered. I prayed and prayed so hard for my mom, and still she was sick, and she suffered. For years I thought Heavenly Father didn't care about her—about me. I worried I wasn't good enough, wasn't perfect enough for His attention."

I stood up and walked across our small dining room, my arms folded across my stomach. "And then I heard a voice say, 'But she had lived.' So I wrote it down. At first I thought it was just another inspired line in the dialogue." I turned and captured Mike's gaze. "But then Clair had her own 'aha' moment. What if that was the answer to her prayers—to my prayers from all those years ago? In my story, Clair's mother first got sick when she was six, paralleling when my mom was first diagnosed. And, like me, Clair prayed her little heart out, the innocent prayers of a child, but they went seemingly unanswered. I was so angry with God when Mom died. For the longest time I lost my faith in prayer. I mean, what good was a prayer if He wouldn't do a little thing like save my mother?"

I pointed at the computer. "But the words 'She had lived' kept coming back into my head. It wasn't just dialogue between two made-up characters anymore. It was as if Heavenly Father was speaking straight to my heart. Those words were meant for me!"

I walked back over to the window seat, wiping more tears from my lashes, but I didn't sit down. "Think about it. The doctors didn't believe Mom would survive that third operation where they tried to get at the first cancerous tumor, but she did. If she had died when I was six—" I shook my head. "I wouldn't even remember what she looked like, or recall the sound of her voice, but because she had lived for eighteen years after she was first diagnosed, I have so many memories that never would've been there."

I sat down, grasping Mike's warm hands in mine. "My prayers were answered. I was blessed—my family was blessed. It just took two characters in a book to tell me about it."

By Debra Erfert

# Our Faith moved a mountain

"Did you hear Jennifer was in an accident today?" At first, that was all we knew that afternoon at school. We weren't surprised. Jennifer was a high-energy, constant-motion kind of person. We all thought the accident was just a fender bender, but gradually we heard more of the details from other kids who saw what happened.

Jennifer and two other girls had left the school grounds to eat lunch at the deli of the local grocery store. The store was across the highway from the rest of our small town, so to drive there meant crossing through highway traffic both coming and going.

A large truck had parked on the shoulder of the road next to the store and was blocking the view of the highway. When Jennifer drove her small car out of the parking lot after lunch, she didn't see the semi-truck coming. It smashed right into the driver's side door. Right into Jennifer. Somehow, she was not killed instantly, but she was left with multiple injuries including a broken neck and back, collapsed lungs, and a ruptured spleen with severe internal bleeding. The other girls' injuries were much less severe.

Our school was small. There were only thirty-three of us in our graduating class that year, and all of us were friends. Jennifer was a beloved and valued member of my senior class and was captain of the speech and debate team. We felt stunned and helpless, so we did the only thing we could think of. We prayed for her. Our teachers even let us pray in school because of the seriousness of the situation, and because we were all so worried and upset. It was hard to think about anything else.

Jennifer was in the intensive-care unit in a hospital an hour away. Her parents stayed there with her day and night. Her friends and classmates were told not to come to visit because we wouldn't be allowed into the ICU, and all we would be able to do is hang out in the waiting room. One of Jennifer's best friends, Samantha, still made the trip regularly and kept the rest of us updated. For quite a while, it didn't look good. Even if Jennifer lived, she could be paralyzed and might not even be able to talk.

As individuals, and at home with our families, we prayed fervently night and morning, thanking the Lord that Jennifer was even alive, and praying that she would recover from her injuries. This was a definite trial of our faith, but we knew if it was the Lord's will, she would make it through.

Then the first breakthrough came. We were sitting in class when Samantha sent a text, and word spread like wildfire. Jennifer had responded to pain stimulus on the bottom of her foot, which meant she was not paralyzed. We all jumped out of our seats and hugged each other and laughed and cried. We were so happy for such a small amount of progress.

Over the next few weeks, Jennifer was able to squeeze her mother's hand and even open her eyes. Every bit of progress was a miracle to us, considering how badly she had been injured. Eventually she started responding to others. She couldn't talk because of her lung injuries and the tracheotomy tube in her throat, so she used sign language.

Now, Jennifer can walk with help, and her lungs are improving. Our class is so grateful our prayers have been answered. It was like God moved a mountain for us because of our faith. Jennifer survived. She still has a long way to go, but we know that if we continue to have faith and keep her in our prayers, the Lord will help her and she will continue to grow stronger.

By Sarah M. Smith

# Left Behind

One day when the handcarts stopped briefly, I went a little way off and lay down on a rock for a minute to rest. I must have fallen asleep. Suddenly, I awoke and wondered where I was. The sun was low. The carts were gone, and it was fast becoming night.

A wolf howled. Was it coming to get me?

What about Indians? What if they were lurking nearby, ready to kidnap me? What should I do?

I said a desperate prayer. I knew God was the only one who could help me.

A horseman came into view. It was a white man, and he was just as surprised to see me.

"Well, little lady, what are you doing out here all alone?"

"I fell asleep, and my friends traveled on without me."

"I need someone to cook and care for me," he said. "You could come home with me."

"No!" I replied. "After all I have sacrificed for the gospel of Jesus Christ, I am not going to quit now. I'm going to Zion, or I will die trying."

"I met your band today. Come, get on my horse with me, and I will take you to them," he said.

We hurried back along the trail and reached camp while it was still light. My new friend left me there with a coin to help me on my way. God had answered my prayer.

By Rose Scoresby; adapted by Marilyn O. Diehl

# The Faith to Ask

*Faith is not to have a perfect knowledge of things; therefore if ye have faith ye hope for things which are not seen, which are true.* (Alma 32:31)

When my mother first got cancer I wanted to pretend as if nothing had changed, as if it really wasn't happening. But it was happening, and I didn't know what to do. I was reluctant to ask for help from anyone. But the bigger problem was that I was forgetting to ask the Lord. By then you would think I would have turned to the Lord, but being me, I didn't.

The day I really freaked out was when Mom started losing her hair. I couldn't take it. I walked out of the house and went to see my Young Women leader, and we just talked. I don't remember everything we talked about, but I do remember her telling me to pray and talk to the Lord. It was then I realized I had forgotten to talk to the Lord during my mother's entire illness. That night I got down on my knees and prayed that my family would be strong and that my mother would be stronger. I've prayed many times since.

Now I feel that however this turns out, the Lord will help me and my family deal with it. Having faith no matter what your trial is and having faith in the Lord—and believing He can work miracles—is the only way to get through your troubles and to gain from your trials. I always walk with God, because when I walk with Him I walk for miles. I know the gospel is true and I love the Lord. I will always turn to Him in faith when life feeds me more than I can chew.

By Catarina Mae Mott

DIVINE NATURE

Be partakers of the divine nature. . . . Giving all diligence, add to your faith virtue; and to virtue knowledge; and to knowledge temperance; and to temperance patience; and to patience godliness; and to godliness brotherly kindness; and to brotherly kindness charity.

–2 Peter 1:4–7

# A mother's Guidance

As a single mother of three sons, one of the things I most wanted to teach them was the importance of prayer . . . not just the "asking" but the "thanking" part, too. Each night as they went to bed they were to think of at least five things they were thankful for that day. Some days they were pretty basic like food, shelter, family, friends, etc. Other times they were more in depth, relating to a certain event that happened that day. My oldest son and I had a rather rough time one particular day, and that night he said in his prayer, "Heavenly Father, I'm thankful I don't have TWO moms, because one is all I can handle!"

Many years later, that same son was playing baseball at BYU and had come home for an extended weekend. He had gone with his brothers to the baseball field at their old high school to practice, and before swinging the bat he took off his CTR ring. This ring had been given to him by his grandmother when he left for college.

When they came home that night, he realized he had lost his ring somewhere on that baseball field. It was dark, it was raining, and it was a big field. He was leaving the next day to go back to school, and he was really upset because this gift from his grandma meant a great deal to him.

After spending time lamenting the loss and searching through his bat bag again and again to make sure the ring hadn't been overlooked, we were certain the ring was gone for good. However, his little brother, who was six at the time, came out of the pantry with four flashlights and wanted to go look one more time. He said a prayer before we all piled into the car and asked Heavenly Father to help us find his brother's ring. It was such a simple, heartfelt prayer by a little boy who loved his brother and hated to see him sad. I was not excited about the prospect of getting absolutely drenched as we walked around the entire baseball field with small flashlights looking for the proverbial needle in a hay stack, but we were all willing to give it a try.

We drove through the rain with the wipers barely keeping up with the downpour, and as we rounded the corner to the ball field, there in front of us on the road was something glistening in the car's headlights. I knew it couldn't be that easy so I figured it was probably a piece of broken glass or a pull tab from a soda can.

But my six-year-old son, with the absolute faith of a child, shouted, "Stop, Mom!" He unbuckled his seatbelt and opened the car door, and right in the middle of the street, shining brightly enough for all to see, was the lost CTR ring!

In that moment I was reminded that it is not enough to simply pray—you have to believe that your prayers are actually heard and answered. Although I had been teaching my sons the importance of prayer, in that moment they taught me the power of faith in prayer.

By Barbara Ericsson

# The Lei

It was my daughter's first birthday since her daddy and I had divorced. I wanted to make it special, both to show her that she was the greatest kid in the world and as proof—to both her and me—that we could make it on our own.

Ann was turning seven and I knew she longed for a special dress, so I took her to a popular clothing shop for kids at the Pearlridge Shopping Center. Money was tight since my divorce, so I browsed through the sale rack. I spotted a dress I thought she would like—one that I could afford. Excitedly, I turned and saw Ann stroking the soft, white collar of a two-piece outfit. She held the dress close to her small body as she gazed into the full-length mirror. She whirled around, caught me staring, and blurted, "Look, Mom!"

The outfit was lovely, with a bed of dainty, pale pink flowers strewn throughout the bodice and skirt. My fingers slid down the plastic thread that held the price tag. I opened my palm. The cost was $35. I had only $15.

"It's closing time, ma'am," the clerk said.

There wasn't time to explain why I couldn't purchase the dress Ann wanted, and I groped for the right words. "We'll come back another day," I managed to respond. The words sounded hollow and empty.

As we stepped from the lights of the shopping center, tiny fingers crept softly into mine until our hands clasped firmly. This was our secret way to say "I love you" when words would not come.

My mind wandered in the quiet night. *How did I come to this place in time?* I thought. *I never imagined that one day I'd be a single parent faced with a situation like this.* A slight tug on my hand brought my thoughts back to the parking lot. It was Ann's way of saying, "It's okay." We smiled and swung our clenched hands.

At that moment, I knew I had to find a way to get that dress.

And so, when my friend Muriel told me the grand prize for the annual city lei contest was $100, I decided I was going to learn how to make a lei. I watched as Muriel expertly braided each fern and flower and knotted off the finished haku-style head lei. It was magnificent! The contest would be held in three weeks. Even though she warned me that professional lei-makers were regular entrants of the big event, I didn't care. I was determined to begin.

I knew I couldn't fly to the Big Island to gather indigenous flowers and ferns, nor could I afford to purchase costly flowers. I would have to find my own materials. So each day during my lunch hour, I scoured the neighborhood, plucking greens and flowers from the gardens of friends. I stored them in plastic bags and took them home. After Ann drifted off to sleep at night, I laid out my day's collection and began experimenting.

Day in and day out I searched and plucked, and night after night I wove and wound until my raw fingers cracked and bled. Finally, less than a day remained in which to create my entry. The fridge was filled with flowers and greens, but I hadn't a clue what to do.

By late afternoon, the whole idea seemed hopeless and far-fetched.

Discouraged, I went to pick up Ann from her after-school program. "Wait, I'm not finished yet!" she pleaded, halfway through a game.

As I sat next to the sandlot, I noticed something small and silvery protruding from the hibiscus hedge. Up close I saw that it was a small hibiscus bud. The tightly wound tip was covered with a fine, silvery fuzz. Then I noticed hundreds of buds scattered throughout the hedge, some large and deep mauve, while others were tiny with only a hint of pink. I picked a few and placed the buds side by side on my lap. Suddenly, I had an idea. I snapped assorted sizes from the branches before the game was over, and then Ann and I headed home.

That night, after my daughter's bedtime story, I reached into the fridge, took out the cool buds, and began winding. I started with the tiny ones and graduated to the full dark ones on the brink of blooming. A huge rosette—made of fuchsia mountain apple calyx, mottled hibiscus leaves, dark green leather ferns, and fine, slivery strips of protea leaves—was joined next to the largest of the swollen buds.

After hours of winding and twisting, the hat lei was complete! I set it to rest in the coolness of the fridge.

The next morning I rushed over to O'ahu's Kapi'olani Park, the site of the competition. At the entrants' table, I was asked to place my creation in a hollow banana stump. The judges peered in and muttered the strange-sounding names of various materials used in the lei. They handed me a number and turned their attention to the next competitor.

Looking around, I noticed the richness and vibrancy of the other lei, filled with extravagant anthuriums, regal white lilies, perfect rosebuds, and powder blue hydrangeas. Embarrassed by my common hibiscus lei, I took one more look at it and left for work.

During my lunch hour I rushed back to the park, eager to see the results of the contest. I leaped from the car and ran into the lei display area.

My heart pounded as I ran searching for my lei. I scanned the rows, but couldn't find it.

*What happened?* I said to myself. *It's not here. It probably fell apart!*

Slowly I made my way back to the car, too ashamed to ask anyone. But as I reached the exit, I decided I couldn't leave without one last look.

This time I walked carefully past each lei. I veered around a group of people huddled around one of the entries. Pausing, I turned, squinted between the crowd of heads, and there it was! I almost didn't recognize it, perched on a light straw hat with a slight tilt to the brim. I stood immobilized. It was breathtaking! A large blue ribbon was tacked next to it with the words "Mayor's Grand Prize" boldly written on it.

Of course, you know the rest of the story. For the very first time since my divorce, I was able to buy a dress for my daughter. I was able to purchase the beautiful pale pink dress with my winnings.

Ann looked as beautiful wearing it as I'd imagined. As she beamed at me, I knew for certain what she had never doubted: With a lot of love and a lot of ingenuity, we were going to make it just fine.

By Linda Tagawa

# Something about Me

*Arise and shine forth, that thy light may be a standard for the nations.* (Doctrine and Covenants 115:5)

My sister Ali and I decided to try out for season five of *America's Got Talent.* We love to sing and we live close to Portland where the auditions were being held. We each prepared a song, but when the judges found out we were sisters, they said they wanted a sister act and that we should try out together. We didn't usually sing together publicly, probably because of the difference in our ages—at the time, I was thirteen and Ali was twenty. We decided to sing "The Climb" by Mylie Cyrus, because we had already practiced it together to sing at our sister's funeral earlier that year. The song also went well with our story.

There are four children in our family, and we all have cystic fibrosis. When we were little our parents were told we might not live long, and that it was unlikely any of us would ever have children. We certainly would not be able to sing professionally as our mother did. Our family has definitely proved the doctors wrong. Singing is an important part of our lives. My mother taught singing, and it seemed like we always had students in our house. Mom formed a singing group called Singers on Stage (SOS), and we were part of it. Our parents encouraged us to take advantage of every opportunity we could.

Our older sister, April, who also enjoyed singing, got married and had two children. My parents hadn't expected to be able to have grandchildren.

Our brother Shaun decided he liked golfing better than singing. He went after it with the same dedication Ali and I put into our singing, and he is now one of the best young golfers in Idaho.

Our parents encouraged us to try out for and participate in everything we could. In 2006 Ali was named first runner-up and Miss Congeniality to Miss Idaho's Outstanding Teen. In 2008, she was chosen as Hero of the Month by Cystic Fibrosis Heroes of Hope. She was a cheerleader and homecoming queen in high school, while maintaining high grades. She studied broadcast journalism at Brigham Young University–Idaho and enjoyed the experience of living with five roommates. Through the years, Ali has had many other opportunities with her singing. She opened for Tracy Byrd and Josh Gracin, and as a little girl, she yodeled in the preshow for the Rosie O'Donnell show. Ali won the KUPI Colgate showdown, won the Boots Competition in Montana, and was named Idaho Idol 2009. Of course, the cause she is most involved with is cystic fibrosis.

When our sister April died at the age of twenty-five, we were naturally very shaken up. Ali had planned to compete in the Miss Idaho Falls pageant that year. She knew April would want her to go ahead, so she did—and she won. Her platform was disability awareness.

Because I'm the youngest, I haven't had as many opportunities yet. I thought being on *America's Got Talent* would help me catch up.

After the Portland auditions, Ali and I were on our way to Las Vegas for the next stage of the competition, then to Hollywood. Before we knew it we were at the semifinals, standing on stage hearing the announcer say: "From Idaho Falls, Idaho, please welcome Christina and Ali!"

It was scary and fun, and soon we were standing there waiting for the judges' comments. Howie Mandell and Sharon Osbourne commented, and then it was Piers Morgan's turn. He has a rough exterior but is the sweetest man, and he became our favorite judge. Our hearts sank as he said, "It wasn't great—I'll be honest with you. It was very nice. I don't honestly think you're the best singers we have. I haven't felt that from the start." Then he added, "But every time I try and buzz you, your big eyes look back at me and you [meaning I] hit the big note . . . "

Next, Piers made the statement that inspired one of our new songs: "There is something about you which is incredibly likeable, and you are inspiring. And so I just love the fact you're here, and for that reason I salute that performance."

We were elated. We made it to the top ten and went on tour with the other nine. What a great experience! Since then, Ali and I have been co-writing songs with writers and producers from Nashville and LA, making recordings, and performing. Since I'm still in high school, I spend most of my spare time doing schoolwork. Ali often speaks to youth groups at firesides.

Our new song, "Something about Me," tells people that no matter what troubles or difficulties they face, there's something about them. There's more to them than just their problems. We now have a five-song EP on iTunes, and we did a music video for our single "The Same Way."

Ali says, "It's so important to shoot for the stars and realize your dreams. We really believe that disability can be surpassed by the abilities you do possess."

Our daily routine includes lots of medication, exercise, and healthy eating. Singing is great medicine, too. The vocal exercises our mom taught us help a lot. While we are doing what we love, we are keeping ourselves healthy at the same time.

"I believe you should focus on the positives and try to fix the negatives," Ali says. "Living joyfully and dreaming big have made all the difference! Cystic fibrosis doesn't define who we are. We define ourselves. Every single day is an opportunity to make a difference to someone somewhere."

Remember that whatever obstacles you face in life, there is something about you.

By Christina Christensen, as told to Marilyn O. Diehl

# Weak Things Become Strong

I remember the shock on my mother's face when my first-grade teacher told her I was in the slow reading group. "What? Are you sure she needs to be there? Her older brother and sister were in the advanced group." I felt stupid. I didn't even know the groups were divided by abilities. This was the first time I realized how different I was. My mother took my hand as we left the classroom, telling me we'd work on it.

As the years passed, I went from being in the slow group to having one-on-one sessions with the Special Ed teacher to help me cope with a learning disability called dyslexia. I was pulled out of class twice a week, given countless analogies to solve, and sent home with photocopies from tattered Dick and Jane books. While the rest of my class was swimming down the Mississippi with Tom Sawyer and flying across the sea in a giant peach, I was stuck reading first-grade picture books.

I muddled through the rest of elementary, skipping large parts of our in-class reading assignments so I wouldn't be the last one to finish. I'd watch my grandpa lavish musty books from the used bookstore on my older sister and spend hours talking about them with her. I wanted that. And more than that, I wanted the independent knowledge that comes from reading. I didn't want my thoughts and ideas to be dependent on what others told me. Inside my head my mind felt starved for knowledge. It was like dyslexia was a veil preventing me from absorbing all but the simplest of truths.

Finally, just before I turned twelve, my Merry Miss teacher shared Moroni 10:4 with us and challenged us to read the Book of Mormon and pray about it. I think this was the first righteous desire

I had that was in direct conflict with my learning disability. How could a girl who had never read a book cover to cover (not even a Beverly Cleary novel) hope to accomplish such an insurmountable task? Just like someone hikes a tall mountain, slow and steady, with occasional breaks and a zigzag of switchbacks.

Two years. That's how long it took me. I read every day, sometimes just a page. My thoughts drifted with each stumble over the strange words. I don't think I understood a word from 2 Nephi, but I plugged on. I prayed nightly for help. I begged Heavenly Father to make me a good reader. Near the very end I came across a scripture in Ether 12:27: "And if men come unto me I will show unto them their weakness. I give unto men weakness that they may be humble; and my grace is sufficient for all men that humble themselves before me; for if they humble themselves before me, and have faith in me, then will I make weak things become strong unto them."

Reading was my weakness, and when I offered it up to the Lord he gave me the strength to overcome it. I finished the summer before my freshman year of high school. I can still remember the pride, the sense of accomplishment that swelled in my chest. Some might argue that it was the constant practice that made me better, and I won't deny that it helped. But I really don't think I could have done it without the Lord's help. It was the constant, everyday feeling of the Spirit that kept me going, even when I didn't understand, even when at times reading felt physically nauseating.

After that I picked up novels, and if you can believe it, I actually read them for fun. That year I didn't have to skip pages to keep up with the rest of the class. With each book, I read faster and my reading comprehension increased. I finally gleaned enough of what I was reading to keep my attention on the text. I dived into fantasy and science fiction, exploring new worlds. It was like my eyes were closed before but now they were open.

I used to be upset about being dyslexic. I thought life wasn't fair because I had to struggle where others did not. But I was a better person for it. I have a stronger testimony that started in my youth because of it. The Lord accepted my meager offering and blessed me all the more for it. The struggle made me strong. It gave me confidence that I could overcome anything with the Lord's help.

By Sarah Anderson

INDIVIDUAL
WORTH

Remember the worth of souls
is great in the sight of God.

–Doctrine and Covenants 18:10

# Priceless

At first glance you could tell Heather was different. Her lips and cheeks were chapped from open-mouthed breathing, constant watery eyes, and a runny nose. Her body was slightly twisted, her gait was jerky, and her voice was husky and strained. No one anticipated she would enjoy, or thrive, during the seventh-grade storytelling unit. She was included because it was the right thing to do, not because anyone thought she'd gain anything out of it.

While clustered in small work groups, students were led through exercises meant to inspire the sharing of personal experiences. Groups were specifically designed to place students with people they didn't usually hang out with. Heather ended up in a group well beyond her comfort zone, but when she started telling her stories, her group listened. There was a moment when she actually paused in wonder because they were hanging on her every word. Throughout the week the size of the circles grew until the final day of the unit, each person told his or her story in front of the entire class.

Heather had originally announced she wasn't going to take a turn, but after being encouraged by her original group, she took the stage. The class loved her story. They laughed at all the appropriate moments and cheered loudly at the end. Heather beamed.

The closing moment of the unit was a storytelling performance in front of the entire student body. Ten students of the core group of sixty were selected to perform. Heather was one of the ten. It seemed as though the audience held their breath as she took slow and jilting steps towards the stage. A collective gasp rose up from the audience when she almost fell going up the stairs. But Heather kept going. She took a moment when she reached the microphone to look out over the student body. This was a tough audience for any storyteller—kindergarten through eighth grade. But Heather owned the moment. The story she told was of her most embarrassing moment. Her pacing was excellent, her delight in the humor was obvious, and the crowd loved her. When she concluded her story, the audience exploded in applause. Heather smiled from ear to ear, then raised her clasped hands above her head like a champion athlete and soaked it all in.

It was a moment few of us will forget, but I believe the sweetest moment came after school that day. Heather was outside waiting for the bus with a cluster of students surrounding her. They were reveling in her story experience and telling her how incredibly cool she was. There is only one word for the expression on her face—priceless. Everyone had been given an opportunity to see past Heather's disability into her heart. Through the new skills she learned and implemented, she gained an increase in confidence. And everyone who listened to her gained a deeper understanding of the girl behind the disability.

By Teresa B. Clark

# Be Still and Know That I Am God

It had been a really hard week—finals week. But that wasn't the only reason why it had been hard. For many months, I had been dealing with a painful shoulder injury that was affecting my participation in orchestra, the amount of time I could practice my viola, my concentration, etc. Also, I had been dealing with depression and anxiety.

I was taking a Spanish final during the last period of the day. It was Wednesday. I was halfway through the week and halfway through all of my final exams. I don't know why, but Spanish had always been the easiest subject for me. So really, I had no reason to worry, and I figured I would get a perfect score on the test. I was bound to get good grades on my other finals, too. But all of a sudden, I started to worry. *What if I don't do well on this final? What about my other tests? I KNOW I'm going to fail them all! My shoulder hurts so much. What if I can never play the viola again? My lifelong dream of becoming a professional violist and musician will collapse around me!*

On and on my thoughts went. They seemed to be swirling in my head. I was panicking. The thoughts kept coming and wouldn't stop. Soon they were racing through my brain almost before I could comprehend them. I didn't know it then, but I was having a panic attack. The fear and emotional pain I felt was so real. Tears leaked down my face, but I wiped them away before anyone could see. I didn't want anyone to think I was crying about the test.

Out of desperation, I offered a silent prayer. "Dear Heavenly Father, please help me. I'm scared. I don't know what to do. What's wrong with me?" Almost immediately, a voice entered my mind, saying, "Be still and know that I am God." The words were repeated several times. With each repetition, my mind cleared and my heart settled a bit more. I was able to take deep breaths. The panic left me. Heavenly Father was trying to tell me to relax and give my stress to Him. Tears of joy escaped my eyes as I recognized the miracle that had occurred and realized the love my Heavenly Father has for me. I said a silent prayer of thanks. After that, I was able to focus on my Spanish exam.

Looking back, I don't remember what grade I received on that Spanish final, nor do I remember my grades on my other finals, other than that I did well. But I do remember the blessed feeling of happiness and peace I felt when the Holy Ghost whispered those simple yet powerful words to me. I'm grateful for the gift of the Holy Ghost in my life and how it has blessed me. I know the Lord answers prayers, and I know He loves His children. Heavenly Father loves me personally, of that I am sure.

By Whitney Churchill

# Kassie and the Soap

For all of you who think there is nothing special about you, I have a story. Not long ago, I was teaching a class. It was a new semester, and I asked the class members to share their names and something unique about them, as a way of getting to know each other. We listened to each student. Most of the comments were highly entertaining. Then, I came to one young mother. She announced that she had a condition called pica.

I had never heard of it. She explained that when she gets pregnant she craves non-edible things. In her case it's soap. Yes, that's right. Soap! She wants to eat soap, and not just any soap. She craves Irish Spring. The class thought that was hilarious. And then to top it off, Kassie announced that she was expecting. This pica and her diet of soap was a current event.

"You really do eat the soap?" I asked

"No," she said, "I just rub the soap on the box and then chew on the box."

"How does your husband feel about all this?" I asked.

"The first pregnancy he was a little traumatized," she said. "But then he decided to go with it. He rubs it all over his face."

The class just lost it. I laughed so hard tears came to my eyes. That is one clever husband.

I have been unable to forget that story. It keeps coming back to me and warms my heart every time I think of it. I hope you won't mind if I share a principle that came to me from Kassie's story.

We are children of God, and each of us is indeed unique in the full and complete sense of that word. There are things about us that are found nowhere else in the human family, and the closer we get to the God who made us, the more He brings out our individuality. And, I might add, not only has God the Father blessed each of us to be delightfully different, but like Kassie's husband, God knows full well how to take advantage of it.

Moreover, the Lord has taught that society is a composite of unique individuals, each capable of contributing to the benefit of the whole (see 1 Corinthians 12:6-31).

So, go find your own soap and make the most of it, and the rest of us will learn how to rub it on our face.

By Glenn Rawson

# Scarier than monsters

A lot of people were afraid of what awaited them when they entered Dr. Slaughter's House of Terror. I loved the thrill that came with the fear. Some pals of mine had volunteered for the haunted house, and they all really seemed to like it. It was a good cause, too. All of the haunted attraction's proceeds went toward helping the D.A.R.E (drug abuse resistance education) program of Idaho. In addition, my school requires each student to complete fifty hours of community service each year. Volunteering at the House of Terror seemed like the perfect solution.

I signed up that year to play a minor character in the main part of the haunted house. I was excited to start scaring that season. The only problem was that when I got to the house to begin the season, they had already given away my part to the girl that played her last year. I was disappointed, but I agreed to take a different role.

The only thing at Dr. Slaughter's that is more prestigious than the characters is the dance team. They practiced for months before the house even opened and poured countless hours of their own personal lives into entertaining the people waiting in line to get into the haunted house. I thought they were the bee's knees, to say the least. I had never imagined that I'd get to work with them, so when the owners offered me a chance to work up front with the best, I accepted. All I had to do was go out in costume on a bike and ride around while an audio recording of the house rules played over the sound system.

I only knew one of the dancers and was intimidated by the rest of them, so I decided to play it cool. Sadly, as a nerdy thirteen-year-old girl, cool wasn't easy. All the dancers were nice enough, but I stayed pretty quiet all the same. I tried desperately to connect with them without letting them know how much of a weirdo I was. This mainly led to awkward, forced conversations.

My deliverance finally came to me through one of the dancer's younger sisters, who was about my age. We got to talking, and this led to my making little connections with some of the others backstage. I also found my walls were starting to chip away as we all continued talking. I forgot about acting cool and started being myself again. That night I left in a good mood, with a feeling of accomplishment in my heart.

The next day I found starting a conversation a lot easier, even though it was with different people. The rest of the season passed like a breeze. Not by being cool, but by being me. No, I didn't have some great epiphany about realizing how I'm the best me I can be, but I found myself all the same. And in the end isn't that what matters?

By Karley Morgan

# A Heart for mariska

November fourteenth was filled with joy as I held my beautiful new baby girl. She had a nice patch of inch-long hair on the back half of her head. We spent the day cuddling our new miracle and showing her off to all our visitors. Life could not get any sweeter.

I remember looking into her angel face. I was overwhelmed with the feeling that the veil was not drawn all the way for her, not just yet. There was such power and wisdom in her eyes. Even my sister commented it wasn't normal for babies to have such intense eyes.

The only glitch was getting her to breastfeed. The nurse said it was normal for new babies to be sleepy, so we undressed her to try to wake her up. Deep down I thought I was doing something wrong.

The next afternoon they tried a bottle. She sucked eagerly but was sweating in the process. Her nurse thought eating should not cause her to work so hard. When her breathing started to race, they transferred her to the newborn intensive-care unit (NICU). They told us she would only be there for a short time, but we soon learned differently. I jumped up to answer the phone around midnight. I could hear the doctor's exhaustion on the other end.

"Mrs. Anderson?"

"Yes."

"You need to come. Your baby has taken a turn for the worse."

I looked at my loving husband as he watched my face turn from excitement to horror. We dropped to our knees and said a fervent prayer. How could something be wrong with her? She was perfect just hours before.

When we entered the NICU, we saw babies you could hold in one hand. Our normal-sized baby looked like a monster next to the others. We felt blessed she was born at full term. After some initial tests that showed some liver abnormalities, the doctor ordered an echocardiogram to look at her heart. He told us something was very wrong with her heart and that she needed to be life-flighted to Primary Children's Medical Center (PCMC) as soon as the pilot returned.

One nurse told us that kids like this are given three options: surgeries that don't turn out so well, a heart transplant, or letting her pass away. It shocked us to hear we should give up on our precious new baby. As long as Mariska was willing to fight, we would fight for her. At 3:30 a.m. we met with the life-flight staff. With my father unavailable and Sam's parents an hour away, my mother was the only one who could be with us.

At PCMC, Dr. Su told us Mariska had hypoplastic left heart syndrome (HLHS). This meant she was missing the two left chambers of her heart, leaving her with half a heart. She would need three surgeries to "re-plumb" her heart. The first one would happen the following Monday.

Mariska's surgeon, Dr. Hawkins, was the first to offer us any hope for her outcome. He said the first surgery was the riskiest, but there were some people with HLHS who had reached the age of twenty-three without a transplant. We were so glad we had chosen to fight for Mariska's life.

Far away in Iraq, my father was serving in the military. During her first surgery, Mariska appeared to my father while he was sleeping. This is what she communicated to her grandpa.

"My mom chose to have me come to earth even though we knew I would have the problem that I do. It will be okay. I can handle it. Time here on earth is short. It's nothing like heaven time, which is different and longer. I have to get back to Mom now."

I did not know about my father's experience at the time, but it reaffirmed what I already felt. Mariska had a lot to get done on earth, and she was in a hurry to accomplish all she could in her allotted time.

After twenty-eight days recovering from her first open-heart surgery, we brought Mariska home with several medications and a feeding tube. Feedings were exhausting: pumping breast milk, mixing it with formula, pushing it through her tube, and then changing all her clothing when it came rushing back up.

Mariska's second surgery happened when she was five months old. She did well and was home after six days. The final surgery was supposed to "fix" her heart and allow her to do normal things, keep up with the other kids, and not have a bluish tinge to her body. Before the operation they checked her heart function with various tests to avoid any surprises.

When we met with Mariska's cardiologist before the surgery, he told us her overall heart function was down. He submitted her case to the board, consisting of a panel of doctors, so the decision could be made as to whether this procedure was the correct action or if Mariska needed a transplant. She only met five and a half of the ten criteria, making their decision very difficult.

In the end they felt a heart transplant would be best. We met with the twelve wonderful members of the pediatric heart-transplant team. We had the false hope that a transplant would be easier. We were in for a long and difficult road. On June ninth, Mariska was placed on the transplant list, somewhere near the bottom, but otherwise she was almost a perfect candidate to receive a donor heart.

After two weeks on the waiting list she had an offer for a heart, but it was meant for another little one. Sam and I were again brought to our knees seeking strength and understanding through prayer. Our sweet two-and-a-half-year-old was slowing down more and more with each passing day. I started to pray that everything would work out the way it needed to. I needed to prepare myself to accept God's will, even if it meant letting my angel return to her Heavenly Father.

In the middle of my prayer I dozed off. I found myself in a kind of vision. I visualized a time when Mariska appeared to be sixteen or seventeen years old and would need a second transplant. I saw the transplant pager that would alert us when it was time to go to the hospital, and it was beeping. I immediately drove to Mariska's high school and rushed down the hall to her classroom. I peeked in, looked at Mariska, and held up the pager. We both broke into tears and drove together to get her new heart.

After this experience I was filled with peace. I had faith that no matter what difficulties awaited us that year, she would make it through. It brought great comfort at a critical time when our world seemed to be in shambles.

Before Mariska received her miracle heart on July eighteenth, we had met with Dr. Kaza, her surgeon. He reviewed her echocardiogram and said it gave him chest pain just looking at it because her heart was so sick at that time. He walked by the room where Mariska was and asked the nurse, "Are you sure that's the right kid?" He was shocked at how active she was and how well she appeared. It was not what he expected, based on her echocardiogram. He commented, "She's the best heart-transplant candidate I have EVER seen! And she even has pink lips."

After receiving her heart, Mariska seemed to be on the fast track for going home, until the first complication came. She had to be fed intravenously for two weeks. After that, her body began rejecting the foreign heart to such a high degree that she was placed back in the ICU for two weeks. Her blood had to be filtered in an attempt to trick her body to stop attacking the new heart. With all the setbacks, she spent two months in the hospital before she came home.

We celebrated as we took Mariska and her grocery sack full of medications back home. For the next five months she had to stay inside with the exception of doctor visits. With her weakened immune system, even the common cold became a real danger. Mariska's body went into rejection again one year after her surgery, but this time she was treated successfully with medications at home.

Mariska has been a tremendous blessing in our lives and we now know why she came to us with only half a heart. Her love for life, her unconquerable spirit, her optimism through pain and suffering, and her wisdom beyond her years are all divine gifts from her Father in Heaven. She has more "heart" than most people do with hearts that are physically whole. With these spiritual gifts, she brings happiness, courage, and hope to everyone she meets. Her mission on this earth is divine, and she came to fulfill a specific purpose. When I see her scars, I am reminded to be patient, to cherish each day, and to never forget that life is a precious gift from God.

By Melynda Anderson, as told to Michelle Bennett Diehl

# Through a Horse

Through a horse I learned a universal truth: that my Heavenly Father knows and loves me, and that I am of infinite worth. In September 2008, life was as near perfect as it had ever been, until Texas, the horse I've had longer than I've known my husband, got sick. Not the sniffling, coughing kind of sick, but the life-threatening, highly contagious and infectious kind.

Ten days after being diagnosed, Texas exhibited symptoms of colic. She stopped eating and her digestive tract began to fail. The infection that had begun as an external abscess on her chest had gone internal. For three days I watched and worried as her health declined. On the third day, with a honeycomb of abscesses covering her stomach, her system failed her. Repeatedly, she dropped to the ground in pain, only to be pulled to her feet by me or my dear friend, who saw my need and refused to leave me alone that night.

The vet encouraged me to bring Texas into the equine hospital for observation, but I didn't know if I could. Texas didn't trailer well alone—she usually refused to enter, then reared and pawed the wall once she was in. I couldn't risk the health of another horse to keep her company. Plus, Texas worries when she's away from home. I feared moving her might do more harm than good and reserved that as a last resort.

I looked at Texas, who was quivering in pain, and heard the Holy Ghost whisper to my mind, "She's dying." I knew at that moment, if I did nothing she would die.

With my husband out of town, I was alone. My dear friend tended to Texas, keeping her on her feet, since rolling and thrashing can complicate an already serious situation. I rushed to help my kids finish homework and get to bed. All the while I contemplated what I should do.

Texas was suffering—that was obvious. Was it time to let go? I'd had twenty good years with her. That's more than a lot of people get, and the Lord had blessed me with a filly that would soon be old enough to ride. If it was Texas's time to go, He hadn't left me horseless.

I fell on my knees next to my bed and poured out my heart. I loved this horse. I didn't want to lose her. I knew if the Lord would simply cast a thought in my direction, she could be well again. I had great faith in the healing power of my Heavenly Father. But during that prayer, I reconciled my will to His, saying in my heart, "Nevertheless, Thy will be done. Regardless of the outcome I will be grateful for the time I had with her." I expressed gratitude to my Father in Heaven, and in my heart I let Texas go, putting things in His hands.

I rose from my knees with a clear purpose and an unnatural calm. I knew one thing—my horse deserved a chance. I wouldn't give up on her or my Heavenly Father. I would provide the opportunity for her to go to the hospital and get the best care possible. Whether she got better would be up to her and the Lord.

Surely a ministering angel attended me that night. I saw in my mind where my husband had stowed the trailer hitch, and I hooked up the trailer and backed it next to the arena with an ease far beyond my skill level. When I opened the trailer door, my friend said, "I'm going to try to walk her in while I have the momentum." I stepped back and nodded. My jaw fell slack as I watched Texas nearly stepping on my friend's heels in her rush to enter the trailer. Then my horse stood so quietly during the forty-five-minute trailer ride that I wondered if she was alive.

At 1:00 AM, we left Texas in the care of the professionals at Willamette Valley Equine Hospital. Exhausted, I drove home and dropped into bed. I fully expected a call that night telling me there was nothing more they could do, and that she should be put down. Considering her age and the mass of infection covering her stomach, surgery wasn't a desirable option.

The next morning I awoke to my alarm. Surprised, I called the vet. Texas had survived the night, and she would yet survive many more. Seeing her step off the trailer onto my property a week later was a testimony of my Heavenly Father's love. In the grand scheme of things, what did it matter to the Lord if one horse lived or died? But to me it mattered. And for Him to exercise His power to save her was a true act of mercy and a testament of my individual worth.

To this day, the vets still marvel at Texas' survival. It was truly a miracle. I thank the Lord for the opportunity to have gone through that trial so I could walk with angels, because never before or since have I felt closer to my Heavenly Father than I did at that time.

By Kelly Nelson

# The Worth of Souls

I slammed my locker shut, Karen's* words still echoing through my head. "I'm not a Mormon anymore. I don't want to be."

How could she say that? I knew she had been struggling with going to church, and that some of her new friends who ate lunch with us talked about religion in a negative way, but Karen's words still caught me off guard.

For three years, she had been one of my best friends. I remembered the sleepovers, the trips to concerts, the time we'd spent in a performing group together. Never once had I thought something like this would happen.

That night, I knelt beside my bed, churning over everything. I had to do something. The conversations at the lunch table were getting harder to ignore, and the more I sat there saying nothing, the more empty and worried I felt. Sometimes the only thing I could think of to do was walk away. But what about Karen? She had been there for me in the past, and leaving felt like abandoning her.

"Father, what can I do?" I thought of Karen's angry face as I stood by her in the hall. "It hurts to see her like this." As I knelt there crying, a warm peace filled me from the inside out. My tears dried up and I knew what my decision needed to be.

In the following days, I sat with Karen as usual, but when her new friends showed up and the conversation turned, I left without feeling guilty. Weeks passed like this. I prayed for Karen again and again. I still didn't know how to help her, but my choice felt right.

I had one class with Karen—math. During the time the teacher let us work together, Karen and I talked like we used to. One day as we worked, she said something about the way I had been acting. I knew she thought I was being judgmental toward her new friends. For a moment, I didn't know what to say. I usually tried not to bring up lunch, knowing it could start a fight.

I turned away from her, looking down at my math problems but not seeing them. As I sat there, an urgent need to speak spread through me, and my hands began to shake. To my surprise, I knew exactly what I should say, and the words came without my forming them. "I hurt so much for you. I think of all the things we used to do together and when I hear you say things like, 'I'm not a Mormon,' I feel like I've lost a part of you." My tears blurred my view of her face. "I keep thinking of how when we first met, you would say a silent prayer for your food at lunch, even when no one else did. It was an example to me." The words were straight from my heart, but they were not just my own. I knew as I spoke them that they were what the Lord wanted me to say.

Tears filled Karen's eyes, too. The trail of words died out. I had said all I could.

More days passed, and we didn't talk about what happened. I hardly saw Karen. The lunch times were divided and we didn't even have the same lunch period anymore. We did have released-time seminary right after each other, and sometimes we passed in the parking lot. One day she stopped me and put a letter in my hand.

I thought she had forgotten about that day in class, but she wrote that after I said those things to her, she started to think about all the people she was letting down. She wanted to change that. She thanked me for what I said.

I stared at the letter and cried, this time for gratitude. I loved Karen, but I hadn't known what to do. It occurred to me how precious she was to Heavenly Father. He loved her, too. I had tried so many times to reach her, limited by my own weakness. But the Lord knew her. He knew what she needed to hear. The words had come from my mouth, but they were His message for her.

I said a silent prayer of thanks. The Lord had answered my

prayers, and at the same time, given me a glimpse of His love, not only for me, but for Karen as well.

*Name has been changed.

By JoLyn Brown

# Conspiracy Theory

*Author's Note: The story I am about to tell you is true, though the names may be changed so as to not embarrass anyone who is trying to repent.*

"Jenny," I called to my best friend in the school hallway. "You are not going to believe who I have to be Secret Santa for this week," I stated in disgust.

Jenny smiled. She opened her locker and swapped books for her next class, then said, "George." At that, she shut her locker.

I scrunched up my face, confused by her answer. "George? No, I wish it were George." While many would consider him the classic geek, George was actually quite nice and cute for a brain. He was funny too, in his philosophical way. No, it couldn't be someone as easy as George. It was . . . I looked around because, technically, I wasn't supposed to tell anyone. "Caleb," I said in a harsh whisper.

"Hmmph," was all Jenny said before she headed for class. She was not one to get all worked up about things like I was. She kept me grounded—was my voice of reason—and while she couldn't stand Caleb either, she never showed how much his comments and rudeness bothered her.

But I still wanted her to react with me. I ran to catch up to her. "Didn't you hear me? It's Caleb! Of all the people. Doesn't Mrs. Smith know how awful he is to me?" As if I was his only victim. "I shouldn't have to be nice to him. I bet you anything she does know and has purposefully set this up so we can work out our 'issues.'" My hands flew up and made invisible quotation marks in the air. "It's a conspiracy, I just know it."

"I doubt that." Jenny smirked.

"Then what do you call it?" I asked.

"Bad luck!"

I brightened a little. She did understand. We stepped into the classroom.

"Who did you get?" I asked, changing the subject.

"Nope, not gonna tell."

"What?" I asked, exasperated. "I told you!"

"So," she said with a wry smile.

I slumped in my chair. She was going to be good right up to the bitter end. Hmmph!

Throughout the next few days, I went about doing the best I could with surprising Caleb, distracting myself with daydreams of who MY Secret Santa could be. *Wouldn't it be nice if it were Joe Bridger?* I thought. Joe was tall, dark haired, and the most popular kid in school. He was handsome, athletic, looked nice in a white shirt and tie on Sunday, and was kind too, not stuck-up like the popular kids I saw in movies and television. Though he didn't talk much, he always listened with a friendly smile.

Then there was his more outgoing cousin Sean, who was also tall and handsome, with lighter-colored hair. He was a jokester, but usually in fun—never rude or damaging. Yes, either one of those fine boys would make a wonderful Secret Santa. I imagined myself at the dance at the end of the week with Caleb, after revealing that I was his Secret Santa, and then one of the Bridger boys would come over and sweep me away the rest of the night. I could be nice to Caleb for one week if that was the reward waiting for me at the end. I focused on that.

On the night of the dance, I met Jenny and some other friends there. The gym was full. There were even kids there who didn't normally go to dances. We were all excited, but I was a little nervous, too. We all had a fun time until the announcement was made that we were to seek out those we played Secret Santa for and ask them to dance.

I watched as Jenny slipped up to George. He seemed pleasantly surprised. I chuckled. She had told me after all in her sly way.

As I approached Caleb, my heart thudded in my throat, and I

nervously smoothed out my skirt. I said to him in my mind: *Please don't freak out! Please don't run off or roll your eyes or pull a face—otherwise I'll die.* Out loud I said, "Hi! I was your Secret Santa." My voice cracked.

Caleb's friend hooted, "You're kidding!"

Caleb shrugged and smiled sheepishly. He silently took me out on the dance floor. We didn't say a word the whole dance, looking everywhere but at each other.

Finally the dance was over and I pulled away. I looked in Joe Bridger's direction in grateful anticipation. He did not come my way— he preoccupied himself with some other girl. That was when Caleb stepped forward and awkwardly announced, "I was your Secret Santa, too." He looked down at his shoes.

I blinked up at him in disbelief as my dreams of dancing with Joe or Sean dissipated. "You're kidding!" I echoed Caleb's friend. This was most definitely a conspiracy!

He shrugged again and offered his hand, tenderly smiling. I willingly accepted and was less nervous this time. I thanked him profusely for all he did for me and went on and on about how wonderful the bunny was that he left me, how it matched my favorite doll at home, etc., etc., as if he cared. And then I fell silent, biting my lower lip and blinking back the sudden tears.

At the end of the dance, I forced a smile, thanked him again, and speedily left the gym. I was overwhelmed with emotions. I wanted to laugh and cry, yell at him for being such a jerk the past two years, and hug him for being so sweet this week. I chided myself for allowing his punk attitude to ruin this experience for me. Most of all, I felt like I could forgive him because his meanness at school had nothing to do with me. He was just mean sometimes.

That week changed both of us. I was more confident and happy, and he was less of a jerk. Oh, he still had his moments, but there were times when he defended me. To this day, I still have the bunny. If Mrs. Smith wasn't the conspirator, it was God.

By Anna Christine Wilson

knowledge

Seek learning, even by study and also by faith.

–Doctrine and Covenants 88:118

# The Ordeal

Three of my friends and I went tubing on the river this past summer. The trip was supposed to last an hour and a half. Unfortunately, half an hour into the trip, our huge inner tube popped on a giant rock. The river swept us away very quickly, and without an inner tube we were all afraid we would drown. When we were all finally able to stand and gather together, we talked about what we should do. We decided that walking back upstream was not possible because the current was too fast, so walking downstream was our only option. The rest of the trip on an inner tube would have taken us an hour, but on our flip-flop-clad feet over a rocky river bottom, it would take much longer.

We knew there was a road on the other side of the river that we could walk on until it brought us to the nearest town, or until we got to a house where we could get help. But we also knew that because of the deep water and the fast current, if we attempted to cross we might drown. On our side of the river was a steep bank covered in foliage that we couldn't climb up. So, walking along the edge of the river, no matter how rocky it might be, was the best option.

It was starting to get dark, and we all knew that in order to get someplace safe we had to cross the river at some point and get to the road. Eventually we came to a fork in the river where the water was more shallow, even if the current was still very rapid. After another quick discussion, we decided the time was now or never to cross the river before the sun went down. We crossed with much difficulty. Almost every step meant falling down and getting back up. We had to practically bear-crawl against the current.

We finally made it across the river! We all breathed a sigh of relief, and even started laughing about our situation, now that we weren't so scared. We immediately felt better after we got to the road and knew it was now only a matter of time before we came to a house.

After the adrenaline that comes with survival instincts wore off, we all realized how many injuries we had suffered: scrapes, gashes, and MANY bruises. I even discovered a small rock imbedded in the heel of my foot! Even with our injuries, though, we felt better than ever. We were joking about how we were all super women, and how girls camp really did prepare us for real-life situations.

While we were joking around, I let my friends know that when we were stepping over some rocks to cross one of the more treacherous segments of the river, I saw a snake curled up on the ground. One of my friends and I had to cross over that snake while the other two took a different route, and while I was scared, I knew I couldn't make a big deal out of it or we might have panicked and possibly harmed ourselves in the pandemonium. So I kept silent while I crossed over the snake, and it turned out my friend did the exact same thing! She knew she shouldn't say anything so everyone could stay calm, and she is even more afraid of snakes than I am! What a blessing it was that we knew what to do in a scary situation like that.

It is true. Girls camp did prepare us for this experience. We used our knowledge to survive, to work together, to determine the safest journey, to take care of our injuries until we got help, and to have faith that the Lord would help us through the ordeal.

By Sarah M. Smith

# You Already Know

The first time I prayed to know if the Book of Mormon was true, I was a freshman at college. I'd read it several times throughout my life and had always felt I had a testimony of it. Yet I was now at a point in life where I had to make a lot of hard decisions, and I knew it was extremely important to find out, once and for all, if the Book of Mormon was really from God or if I had been deceived my whole life.

After rereading the Book of Mormon, I fasted for a whole day—my first twenty-four-hour fast. Then I knelt by my desk chair to ask God if the book was correct. I can still remember how the light poured in through the window and how nervous I was. I was afraid I would get an answer and that I would have to change the way I was living my life. I also think I was terrified that I might not get an answer at all. But I put my fears aside and poured out my heart to God. I told Him what I was struggling with and that I really needed to know if the Book of Mormon was from Him.

At first, I didn't get an answer. In fact, I remember thinking I should just get up off my knees because I was being ridiculous. Then a beautiful sense of peace washed over me and a still small voice spoke to my soul, saying, "Heather, you already knew it was true." The truth of those words enveloped me, and I knew that I did know and that the wisdom and power of the Book of Mormon had blessed my life over and over. I didn't need any further witness.

What I felt that day changed the focus and direction of my life. I can confidently say that the Book of Mormon has been the most influential book in my life. Through it my testimony of the Bible has been strengthened, as has my love and understanding of my Savior

Jesus Christ. If you haven't ever read the Book of Mormon, you are missing out on one of the world's greatest treasures.

By Heather Farrell

# The Obstetrician

"Mama, a snake bit me," I screamed.

"Tom, come quick! A rattler just bit Sally!" my mother yelled.

I saw my father race past. Where was he going? In minutes he was back, carrying a squawking chicken. As soon as Father reached me, he cut the chicken open and thrust my foot inside.

"Tom! What are you doing?" my mother cried.

"Something I learned from the Indians, Harriet. This will pull all of the poison out and save Sally's life."

We were some of the first settlers in Tooele, Utah, and even though my father had no formal training, he was the best doctor around at that time. People often called on "Father Tom," as he was called, when there was sickness or an accident. He had a natural ability for healing and had learned all kind of remedies from the Indians and from my grandmother. It wasn't long before I was old enough to accompany him and help out. I enjoyed learning all I could.

One of my brothers had a serious accident and shattered his leg. Father set it so well that my brother didn't even walk with a limp. When Father broke his jaw, he stood in front of a mirror and set it himself.

When Joseph Rowberry asked me to marry him, I happily accepted. We were to be married October 28, 1866. There was so much work to be done that I still had a load of sugar cane to strip when Joe drove up behind a beautiful horse hitched to a new cart, which was a luxury at that time. Joe was so understanding. He changed to work clothes borrowed from my brother and helped me finish. For a wedding present he brought me a beautiful pair of high-topped shoes. This was my first pair of shoes that were not homemade. I felt like the most fortunate girl in the world.

After we were married we went to our home in Erda, where I started milking cows and making butter and cheese. I felt like the world was mine.

Our first little girl was born prematurely, but she was doing well until she got sick and died from whooping cough before she was three months old. I felt it was my fault. If I could save the children of others, why couldn't I save my own child? But life had to go on, and Joe was so good and kind to me.

We had five more children, and when the baby was about one, our lovely little five-year-old, Johnny, fell off a wagon. His head was crushed under a wagon wheel. They rushed him to me, but neither Father nor I could do much for him, and we knew as much about medicine as anyone else in the valley at that time.

"Mama, help me," Johnny begged for three days before he died. My beautiful black hair turned gray from grief. All these years later, I still can't talk about it without a sob in my throat.

About 1893, I was called by the Church authorities to go to Salt Lake to take schooling in obstetrics and child care from Dr. Ellis Shipp. I had been doing this work for many years, but now was my chance to learn more and better ways. I was so grateful for this opportunity.

I practiced all over the Tooele Valley until 1903, when I was called by the Church to go to Iona, Idaho, where they needed trained obstetricians. By this time Joe and I had sixteen children. He had suffered a stroke a few years before this, but we decided to move with the few children we had left at home.

I always wore a black dress and a large, white, starched apron and I always made it a point to wash my hands thoroughly before attending a patient. I was very busy and in demand constantly, night and day. When I was set apart for this work, I was promised I would always be blessed with health and wisdom in my work, if I would keep my covenants and my faith.

Anytime I had a call, I would go, no matter what time of night or day and in spite of the weather. When I would hear a horse coming at a fast pace down the road, I would hitch up my horse, Coalie, to the cutter and be ready to go, sometimes for many miles. I would hear the young boys calling to each other, "Tom, Billy, Jack! Let's follow Aunt Sally and see who is having a baby now."

Sometimes I had to spend the night with my patient. They all received the best of care from me personally. Those who needed help called if they had access to a phone. For example, when Susie Armstrong started having problems, she called to her daughter, "Mary, get the dishtowel and go to the top of the hill and wave it until your sister sees it, so she can get to the store and telephone Aunt Sally. I need help now!" This was one of those times I had to treat a woman after a "medical doctor" attended her. Some of those doctors simply could not be convinced of the necessity of washing their hands between patients.

I delivered fifty-seven of my own grandchildren. I have records of more than two thousand babies that I delivered.

By Sarah (Sally) Jane Lee Rowberry; adapted by Marilyn O. Diehl

# Portuguese Prayers

While I was serving a Spanish-speaking mission in Washington, D.C., my companion and I saw an older woman walk up her porch steps, glance at us, and then go inside. My companion looked at me and said, "You want to go talk to her, don't you?" I grinned and nodded, and we walked to her door.

I began with our standard door approach in Spanish. "Nos gustaría compartir un mensaje acerca de Jesucristo." ("We would like to share a message about Jesus Christ.")

As I said Christ's name, the woman's face lit up. "Por favor, venha dentro," she said, inviting us in. She was speaking Portuguese. We introduced ourselves and she said her name was Alzira. Miraculously, I was able to understand what she said—and she could understand me! For me, this opportunity was an answer to months of fervent prayer and study.

At the beginning of my mission, I served with an Argentinian sister. We spent hours knocking on doors, looking for people who might be interested in the message of the restored gospel of Jesus Christ. We met a woman named Angelica who had come from Brazil to receive treatment for a large tumor that had spread to several parts of her body. I understood her only through sign language and her showing us the tumor and scars. The Portuguese went right over my head. This woman had incredible trust in God. Unbelievably, the tumor had stopped growing. Her cancer cells were being studied and analyzed at Johns Hopkins Medical Center. Her doctors were amazed, and she was grateful for this wondrous healing and second chance at life.

My companion spoke enough Portuguese to explain our belief in a loving Heavenly Father who hears our prayers, and that through

His mercy He has once again called a prophet to guide His children. We had a DVD of the Restoration with Portuguese audio, and we watched it with Angelica. She accepted our message and agreed to have us come again.

Because of the language barrier, it was difficult to set up another appointment. It broke my heart that we lost touch with Angelica, and we learned that she returned to Brazil. I prayed she would be led to the Church in her own country, and vowed to never let something like that happen again. I needed the gift of tongues!

That chance came at New Year's. I was transferred to a new area, where the Relief Society set a goal to read the Book of Mormon before the anniversary of the organization of the Relief Society in March. I realized this could be my chance to study the Book of Mormon in Portuguese. It was frustrating at first. The language was close enough to Spanish to make me think I knew what was being said, but different enough that I had to look up the phrases in Spanish *and* English to fully understand. My progress was slow, but that just encouraged me to rely more on the Lord and continue studying.

I prayed constantly: "I know there are people who need to hear Thy teachings in Portuguese. I want to learn this language so badly. I promise that if Thou wilt help me to learn it, I will do my best to find those people and help them. Please bless me to understand. Please bless me to be able to teach in Portuguese."

I was about halfway through O Livro de Mórmon when we met Alzira. At that time she was studying another religion, but she didn't agree with its teachings. She was upset by all the problems she was having in her life. She cried as she told us how she lived alone and sometimes went for days without talking to anyone but her dogs. This was someone who desperately needed to feel God's love in her life.

We taught Alzira a little bit about the Book of Mormon and Joseph Smith, and we invited her to come to church. She could see that what we had was good and was willing to give it a try. We returned that week with a member who had served in Brazil. He really helped us out for a couple of lessons.

I was still studying O Livro de Mórmon daily and praying that the Lord would help us to be able to communicate with this sweet woman. I would practice speaking with the Brazilian sisters in the visitors' center, watch the Mormon Messages in Portuguese, and study the Portuguese subtitles as I watched the *Preach My Gospel* DVDs. My companions caught the spirit, and we all started learning. Alzira appreciated our efforts to teach her in her own language. She would explain words to me, and I would write them down in my planner.

Alzira began coming to church and was baptized a month after we met her. In the power of prayer and faith, she found the remedy for her frustrations and peace for her troubled heart. She said later that she considered me and my companion *seus anjos do céu*—her angels from heaven.

I am so grateful for the gift of tongues and the miracle of inspired prayers. "And whatsoever ye shall ask the Father in my name, which is right, believing that ye shall receive, behold, it shall be given to you" (3 Nephi 18:21). It's interesting—I was an answer to Alzira's prayer, and she was an answer to mine.

By Leah Anderson

# Piano Music

There are advantages and disadvantages to coming from a large family. Make that a large family with a single parent, and they double. My mother knew she could not send me to school and pay for it. She worked in a retail store and made just enough to pay the bills and take care of the other children at home. If I wanted to go to college, it was up to me to find out how to get there.

I found that I qualified for some grants because of the size of our family, my mom's income, and my SAT scores. There was enough to cover school and books, but not enough for room and board. I accepted a job as part of a work-study program. While not glamorous, it was one I could do. I washed dishes in the school cafeteria.

To help myself study, I made flash cards that fit perfectly on the large metal dishwasher. After I loaded the racks, I stood there and flipped cards, learning the makeup of atoms while water and steam broke them down all around me. I learned how to make $y$ equal to $z$ while placing dishes in stacks. My wrinkled fingers flipped many a card, and many times my tired brain drifted off and a glass would crash to the floor. My grades went up and down. It was the hardest work I had ever done.

Just when I thought the bottom was going to drop out of my college career, an angel appeared. Well, one of those that are on Earth, without wings.

"I heard that you need some help," he said.

"What do you mean?" I asked, trying to figure out which area of my life he meant.

"Financially, to stay in school."

"Well, I make it okay. I just have trouble working all these hours and finding time to study."

"Well, I think I have a way to help you."

He went on to explain that his grandparents needed help on the weekends. The person would need to cook the elderly couple's meals and help them get out of bed in the morning and into bed in the evening. The job paid four hundred dollars a month—twice the money I was making washing dishes. I went to meet his grandparents and accepted the job. Now I would have time to study!

My first discovery was my friend's grandmother's love of music. She spent hours playing her old, out-of-tune piano. One day, she told me I didn't have enough fun in my life and took it upon herself to teach me to play. My campus had several practice rooms with pianos where musicians could practice. I found myself going into those rooms more and more often.

Grandma was impressed with my ability and encouraged me to continue. Weekends in their house became more than just books and cooking; they were filled with the wonderful sounds of the out-of-tune piano and two very off-key singers.

When Christmas break came, Grandma got a chest cold, and I was afraid to leave her. I hadn't been home since Labor Day, and my family was anxious to see me. I agreed to come home, but for two weeks instead of four, so I could return to Grandma and Grandpa. I said my goodbyes, arranged for someone else to temporarily care for the couple, and returned home

As I was loading my car to go back to school, the phone rang.

"Daneen, don't rush back," my friend said.

"Why? What's wrong?" I asked in a panic.

"Grandma died last night, and we have decided to put Grandpa in a retirement home. I'm sorry."

I hung up the phone feeling like my world had ended. I had lost Grandma, and that was far worse than knowing I would have to return to dishwashing.

I went back at the end of four weeks, asking to begin the work-study program again. The financial-aid advisor looked at me as if I had lost my mind. After I explained my position, he smiled and slid an envelope across the desk. "This is for you," he said.

It was from Grandma. She had known how sick she was. In the envelope was enough money to pay for the rest of my school year and a request that I take piano lessons in her memory.

I don't think "The Old Grey Mare" was ever played with more feeling than it was my second year in college. Now, years later, when I walk by a piano, I smile and think of Grandma. She is tearing up the ivories in heaven, I am sure.

By Daneen Kaufman Wedekind

CHOICE AND ACCOUNTABILITY

Choose you this day whom ye will serve . . . but as for me and my house, we will serve the Lord.

—Joshua 24:15

# In a Pickle with a Peach

It was the perfect peach—ripe, warm, juicy. I savored every bite, even licking my fingers. I open the screen door and let it go, too late to stop it from banging.

"Afton?" There was a hint of annoyance in my mother's voice. I shoved the pit to the side of my mouth and wiped my face on my sleeve.

"Sorry if I woke you."

"Well?"

I was sure I was in trouble, though I wasn't sure why. I spit out the peach pit, "Peach juice," I answered after spitting out the pit.

"And where did the peach come from? You know what I told you about taking something from a stranger."

"Oh, no. No one gave it to me—I picked it myself." I hesitated. "Off a tree."

Mother finished washing my face—firmly—and rinsed the cloth.

"Our next-door neighbors don't have peach trees, either." She made that "well maybe you better show me" sound and held out her hand.

We walked down the alley until we came to the last house. They had a high white fence, and towering above was a beautiful tree, loaded with peaches. "See? Up there." I pointed.

Mother agreed it was a lovely tree, then said, "None of the branches hang over the fence. How did you reach one?"

"Oh, easy. I climbed on the garbage can and then the fence, and from there I could reach the tree." I explained, proud of my agility. I knew the sudden silence was not good.

"Want me to show you?"

The silence thickened. Then mother turned me around.

"You trespassed in a strangers' back yard, climbed over a privacy fence, and stole a peach?" the words came out like a drum beat.

"It was just hanging there, and there are so many. I just picked it. That's not stealing, that's just taking."

From the look on Mother's face, I knew I had done something bad and she was not happy with me.

"Stealing is taking something that isn't yours without paying for it or asking permission," she announced.

"No one was home, and the tree can't talk." I tried to laugh it away, but it didn't work.

"You have to tell them what you did." She reached out for my hand. "It is important that we be good, honest neighbors."

"I can't give it back. I ate it. You know I don't have any money to pay for it."

"We will find a way," was my mothers' response.

"Are you going to explain for me?" I was desperate now. She shook her head no. That juicy peach turned very sour and heavy in my stomach as mother marched me to the front door and rang the bell.

"Stop fidgeting." Mother patted my shoulder. "We will work it out."

"Work? I don't know how to do any work," I protested.

"You are a pretty good climber. Maybe they need one," she offered as the door opened.

It turned out my mother knew the man inside as Doctor Adams. He invited us in and asked us to sit.

"This is my daughter, Afton," Mother began. "She has a confession to make." She nudged me to my feet and put her hand on my back.

"Oh, is that so? Just what do you need to confess?" asked the doctor.

I gulped. The peach was a lead ball in my stomach now, and the taste in my mouth was bitter.

As I began, I took a deep breath and spoke quickly. "I climbed over your fence and up the peach tree and I took one. I can't give it back because I ate it, and I can't pay money because I don't even have an allowance yet because I am only eight years old. Please don't send me to jail." I could feel the tears filling my eyes as I made my plea.

Mother and the doctor exchanged looks, and both ended up smiling.

"Seems like you are very good at climbing fences and trees . . ." the doctor began.

That is exactly what I did to pay for one peach. For three weeks, I climbed the tree under the cook's watchful eye until every peach was picked. Then we went to the kitchen to slip the skins in very hot water. There were also the hours of preparing the peaches for pies, cakes, jams, and jellies.

My favorite was when we took the smaller ones and pickled them— delicious! Pickled is still my favorite way to fix peaches. The juicy peach was a lesson in making good choices and being accountable for my mistakes, and I have never forgotten it.

By Afton W. Huff

## Pickled Peaches

Cling peaches are best for pickling, but freestone may be used.

2 sticks cinnamon
1 tablespoon whole allspice
1 tablespoon whole cloves
4 cups sugar, divided
2 cups water
3 cups vinegar
24 small, firm, ripe peaches, peeled

Tie spices in a cheesecloth bag. Place spice bag, water, vinegar, and 2 cups sugar in a large pot. Bring liquid to a boil. Add peaches a few at a time. Allow to simmer until thoroughly heated.

Carefully remove peaches and add new ones until all have been heated. Remove spice bag. Place peaches in canning jars and gently press down, being careful not damage peaches. Add remaining 2 cups sugar to syrup mixture and bring to a boil again.

Carefully pour heated liquid over peaches in the jars, leaving ¼ inch head space. Run a knife blade or other straight object down the inside of the jar to release air bubbles. Add more liquid if necessary. Clean top of jars and place caps on jars, then tighten.

Process pints or quarts for 15 minutes in a water bath brought to a boil. Carefully remove jars and allow to cool. Listen for the jar lids to "pop."

Makes approximately 6 pints or 3 quarts. If you are young, let a grownup help you—it's a good choice.

# never too late

I was fifteen. I knew boys were extremely cute, and sixteen just seemed so far away. The girls' choice Sadie Hawkins dance was coming up and all the girls were finding their dates, asking them in creative ways. It all just seemed like a lot of fun—fun I wasn't having and couldn't have for another year. My friends really wanted me to go, which made the temptation even greater.

I was living with my dad (my parents were divorced) and he didn't really care if I dated before I was sixteen. I had a lot of thinking to do. After days of dreaming of how much fun it would be, I decided to talk to my mom about it.

"But Mom, all my friends are going and I'll be the only one left behind," I said, disappointed.

"The choice is up to you," my mom said. "But I would pray about it if I were you."

She then told me a story about how when she was my age she wanted to go to the "Freshman Frolic" and she decided to meet a boy there. The dance was a lot of fun, but that was the beginning of when things we shouldn't do started to be "okay."

I finally decided I didn't want to wait to go on my first date. I wanted to ask a boy named Cody to the Sadie Hawkins dance. But I felt like I needed permission. My dad was just sitting on the couch watching TV like he usually was, and I wanted to ask him about going to the dance.

"Hey, Dad," I said nervously.

"What is it, my Brit?" he asked me tenderly.

My heart started racing and I said, "Oh, nothing."

We walked into the kitchen, and as he grabbed a snack, he said, "Janie said you wanted to ask me something."

I had already talked to my sister about the dance on the phone the previous night, and she probably talked to him about it.

I took a deep breath, nervous as ever, and choked these words out, "Can I ask someone to the Sadie Hawkins dance?"

My dad just laughed, looking at my nervous face, and said, "Yeah, that's fine."

I smiled and began planning everything out, finding a group, and thinking of a fun way to ask Cody to the dance.

After I asked him to the dance, he asked me to be his girlfriend. I couldn't help it, I told him yes. We dated up until the dance, and then we broke up afterwards. Nothing bad happened, but I talked to my mom about the situation, and she told me that it wasn't too late—that I could still wait until I was sixteen to date.

This experience taught me that it's never too late to turn back. Our Heavenly Father would never want us giving up, so I didn't. From that day forward I was going to wait until I was sixteen to date. Easier said than done, but I did it with the Lord's help. I got asked out on dates, but I didn't go because I had made a promise to myself and to the Lord to never turn back. I should've never gone on a date before I turned sixteen, but I learned we can ALWAYS change and do the right thing.

President Heber J. Grant said, "I desire to impress upon the minds of the young [people] that because they have not succeeded in the past, or have failed to live proper lives, they should never feel that there is no hope for them in the future. There is no teaching of our Lord and Master, Jesus Christ, which is plainer than that laid down by him to the effect that there will be none of our past sins held against us, provided we repent and forsake them, in the future laboring diligently for the right" (*Teachings of Presidents of the Church: Heber J. Grant*, p. 39).

I'm happy I decided to stop dating until I turned sixteen, and now I know that the Lord really does work in mysterious ways. And in the end, you always learn that He was right all along.

By Brittany Hannan

# A most Important Decision

My best friend Marta called on New Year's Day 1941. "My cousin Keith is home from his mission," she told me. "My folks said I could take the car and drive out to see him. Do you want to go with me?"

"Of course I do," I exclaimed.

When we arrived at his home, he was getting ready to go on a date.

"But I have time to visit with you for a while," he insisted.

The Saturday after our visit with Keith, I had just donned my sister's ice skates and was preparing to learn to skate on the ice rink my brothers had made by flooding our large garden space, when I was called to the telephone. It was Keith.

"May I come see you?" he asked.

Of course I said yes.

We went rabbit hunting, of all things. Afterward, we went back to Keith's home, where we enjoyed chili the hired man had made. That was the beginning of a rather persistent courtship. Almost every night, when I got off work at the telephone office, Keith would be waiting to meet me, to give me a ride home or take me to a show, a dance, or some other activity, depending on what time my shift ended.

When Keith started talking about marriage, I had some hesitation. "You know I'm helping support my brother on a mission," I reminded him. "I plan to save enough money to go to college and serve a mission myself, and Aunt Sue wants me to stay with her so she can give me vocal lessons."

Keith persevered, saying we could fill a mission as a couple later in our lives, but I needed more time to make a decision. I regularly made it a matter of prayer, and I had faith those prayers would be answered eventually.

Keith was a partner with his parents in the business of fattening pigs and taking them to Omaha, Nebraska, to sell them. During one of these trips, the Idaho Falls LDS Stake was having their annual M-Men and Gleaner (young adult) week, with an activity of some kind every night. During that week, every young man I had seriously dated escorted me to or brought me home from one of these activities. It gave me a chance to compare them to Keith.

On the Sunday evening that concluded these activities, a meeting was held, with Elder Oscar A. Kirkham of the First Council of the Seventy as our speaker. All the young people lined up afterward to have Elder Kirkham sign their programs. Since I was singing in the choir, I was standing in the line behind him. It wasn't my turn, but he suddenly turned around and took my program, signed it, and said to me, "You will choose your husband through faith in God and love of nature."

Since this definitely described Keith, I had my answer. On our first date after he came back from Omaha, I told him I was ready to marry him in the temple—as soon as my brother returned from his mission.

It was a comfort to know Heavenly Father approved of my decision, and I've never regretted it during the seventy years since. I'm looking forward to being with Keith in heaven.

By Beth R. Olsen

# Free to Choose

"Young lady!" boomed a voice overhead.

My feet stopped and my heart skipped a beat. I turned around to see the store clerk looming over me, his head and shoulders blocking the late afternoon sun pouring through the mini-mart windows, his arms sternly folded across his chest.

"Yes?" I squeaked in my seven-year-old voice.

"Hand it over!" he demanded, stretching his palm toward me.

I nervously moved the item around in my pocket. "I don't have anything," I lied.

"Give it to me!" This time he shouted. Not only was I stealing from him, I was lying right to his face, and he knew it.

I pulled the small pack of gum out of my pocket and handed it to him. He snatched it out of my hand in disgust and forcefully marched me up to the front of the store, where my parents were waiting to check out. I was scared to death. They were going to kill me! Or worse, I would get a good tongue-lashing.

"Please, sir, I was going to pay for it. Honest! Please let me go and I won't do it again."

Of course he didn't believe me. "Is this your daughter?" the clerk asked my father.

"Yes," my father replied, obviously concerned.

The clerk proceeded to explain to my father what had happened—how he saw me take the gum, how I lied about it, and how, if my father didn't do something about it, my family and I were no longer welcome in his store. I watched as my Dad's face changed from shock to embarrassment to rage. Mother kept her eyes to the floor or on my two restless younger brothers beside her.

My father profusely apologized and quickly paid for the items he came for, then turned to me. His steely eyes penetrated my very soul. "To the car—now!" he barked.

Then something worse than death or a tongue-lashing happened as punishment. Silence. Dead silence, except for the whispers from my curious, speculative brothers. My parents were so angry or upset that they didn't know what to say. What punishment would fit this crime? Hadn't they taught me better than that? Why would I need to do such a thing? My excuse was that they wouldn't buy me the gum. They didn't like it—said it was bad for my teeth. So I took it. What did it hurt, anyway? It was only twenty-five cents. This was how I justified myself all the way home.

When we got there, I was sentenced to hard labor. Mom carried our purchases and led my brothers into the house, while Dad stomped off to the tool shed. He came out with the old-fashioned, rusty, push lawn mower my great uncle had used when he first owned the property. It looked like a mini grain cutter, and you pushed it back and forth to cut the grass because it had no motor. My dad set it out in front of me.

"What do you want me to do with this?" I asked a bit snobbishly.

"Cut the grass," he retorted, pointing to the front lawn.

"But I don't know how," I began to whine. "Why can't I use the motor one?"

"Because I gave you this one. This is as good a time as any to learn." Then he explained how it worked.

It was hard work. Sweat trickled into my eyes in the first two minutes. My arms, back, and shoulders ached from the constant back-and-forth movement. I was out there for a very long time, working halfheartedly so I wouldn't be done too soon and have to face my parents. It was suppertime, and I had few blisters on my hands before I was told to quit. During the next two weeks, I also washed windows inside and out, kept the porch clear of debris, and mowed more of the lawn.

We never talked about the incident much after that, and I never dared bring it up. But the experience is burned in my memory to this day, and I wish I could say I had learned my lesson. But I hadn't. When we moved to a new town, I was an older, wiser ten-year-old and hadn't thought of stealing anything since that day of infamy. But the temptation crept back into my life one fateful day.

This time Dad was not with us when we went to the store, and we had to walk. While Mom searched for items for dinner, I wandered through the candy aisle. In the aisle was a new kind of gum, Bubblicious, bigger and juicier than regular stick gum. My parents still wouldn't buy gum for me or my brothers, but my cousins sometimes shared their gum with me so I knew what it was like.

This time I was able to get the pack of gum out of the store without getting caught. I stealthily unwrapped the wrapper with one hand and popped a piece in my mouth. Mom marched ahead, absorbed in her own problems. My brothers played happily along the way without missing a beat. But when I began to chew the gum, my youngest brother came up to me and said, "Hey, whatcha eating?" Mom didn't hear. She kept on trudging.

"Nothing! Go away," I whispered harshly. My secret was about to be revealed.

"You're eating something. I saw it. I want some!" my little brother persisted.

"No. There's nothing for you to have." My whispering became more desperate.

Defeated, my brother ran off to walk and play with my other brother, and no one else noticed I was chewing gum.

But I was sick. The gum tasted awful in my mouth. There was no way I could enjoy it, not without getting caught. It wasn't worth it to me to go through all that effort just to have a piece of gum or anything else. Even though I never had the guts to confess what I'd done and pay for the gum, I decided right then and there that I was going to be content with whatever I got. I spit the gum out and threw it and the rest of the pack away in a dumpster on the way home. But I still felt guilty. Later I learned it was the Holy Ghost working on me so I would repent.

Eventually, my parents let up on the rule of no gum, and Grandma began to pay me for helping her around her house. When I paid for my own pack of gum a few months later, I felt free.

If I would have listened to the still small voice before I took the gum, I wouldn't have been miserable. Wickedness never will be happiness. You are free to choose, but if you follow the Holy Ghost, He will help you choose wisely.

By Anna Christine Wilson

# Real Friends

"Hi, Micki. I invited Jan to hang around with us at the amusement park tomorrow," I said as we walked down the hall between classes.

Micki blew up. "You what? She's not cool."

I looked at her in surprise. "Come on. She didn't have anyone to go with, and besides, I've been friends with her since elementary. She's lots of fun—you just need to get to know her."

I twisted a strand of my hair as I watched Micki's facial expressions. She was turning almost purple with anger.

"She dresses weird and is a nobody. She'll ruin our image. She can't come with us." Micki glared at me.

I froze, stunned. I had no idea Micki could be this way. What was I going to do? My stomach felt like I'd swallowed an angry humming bird.

Micki and I had met earlier that year when she moved to our high school. Everyone thought she was gorgeous and funny. I was pleased that for some strange reason, she had singled me out to be her best friend.

Now she leaned closer to my face, her eyes narrowed as she said, "You're going to have to choose. If you want to come with us, you need to get rid of her." She fluffed her hair as she turned and marched away.

If I didn't tell Jan she couldn't come with us, Micki would hate me, and I would no longer be a part of the "in" group. But I couldn't do that to Jan because it would be mean. Why did Micki have to be that way? The warning bell rang, interrupting my inner battle.

Micki ignored me at lunch even though we sat by each other at the "popular" table. *Wow, she really meant it. I thought maybe she would say not to worry about it.* I ate my lunch in silence. All day I thought about what

Micki had said and tried to figure out how I could make it work for all of us. I had experienced the pain of not belonging and had spent most of my life on the outside looking in. I didn't want to be the object of the snide glances and snickering again. I wasn't sure what to do and dreaded the next day's end-of-year field trip.

That night Jan called and asked me what I was wearing. Then she began to debate which top would look best with her jeans. She did most of the talking, and she sounded so excited. When there was a lull in the conversation, she said, "Uh, are you listening? I asked you what Micki said when you told her I was coming with you guys."

There it was. I had to make a decision. I said a quick prayer, took a deep breath, and said, "Well . . . she doesn't know you, and so . . ."

Jan broke the uncomfortable silence. "Okay, no problem. Maybe I'll run into you and we can catch a ride or two together."

"Wait! I'm coming with you. You are my good friend and I wouldn't do that to you. It will be just you and me, if that's okay with you." As I felt the tight fist that had been clamped around my stomach all day release, a feeling of peace filled me from head to toe.

This was the right thing to do even if I was no longer part of the popular group and they chose to make fun of me. I didn't like Micki's attitude, and if she was going to be upset about this, maybe she wasn't really a friend after all.

I waited for Jan to say something. Finally, in a quiet voice she said, "Sure, that'll be great. Thank you for being a good friend." Then she added cheerfully, "We're going to have a blast tomorrow."

"Yes, we are. I was thinking, should I would wear my blue-and-white-striped top with my blue hoodie?"

I no longer worried about what the next day would bring. My heart was full, and I knew I had done the right thing.

By Cindy R. Williams

# The Haircut

Getting or not getting a haircut is a matter of life or death, or at least it feels that way to a girl who is desperate for one. I was just such a girl as a missionary serving in Frankfurt, Germany, with my companion Sister Newbury. We lived on the third floor of a twelve-story apartment building near downtown. A park where we liked to walk separated us from the Frankfurt Zoo. It was an exciting place to live.

We were working with a lady, Julia, and her son, Jakob. She was the typical jack of all trades. She did a little bit of everything, including haircuts. After sharing a spiritual message at one of our visits with Julia, we made plans to meet later in the week so that I could have a long-awaited haircut. As sister missionaries we didn't spend a lot of time focusing on what we looked like. There wasn't much money or time for clothes-shopping and makeup. The clothes left behind by other sister missionaries had to satisfy the need for something new to wear. But I had gone my whole mission so far (ten months) without a haircut, and it was time for a change!

After making the appointment with Julia, I was so excited to look different. The big letdown came when Julia called and had to cancel our meeting because Jakob wasn't feeling well. AHHHH! I was so frustrated. Then to top it all off Sister Newbury got sick, and we had to stay home all afternoon and evening instead of working. Sister Newbury was nothing but a bump on her bed after taking her medicine. I was a restless, caged animal, needing something to do. One whole wall of our studio apartment was windows. I had a fabulous view of the city. I sang to my own reflection in the windows—that long-haired girl who needed a haircut. Looking at that girl, I got an idea.

How hard could a haircut be? I began searching for scissors. The selection wasn't the best. One pair looked like it could have come from a preschool. The other, long and pointy, looked the most promising.

The bump on the bed moved as I made my way to the bathroom. "Sister Behunin, what are you doing?" Sister Newbury eyed me. "Um, don't forget to pray about it!" A typical missionary response.

"Sure," I replied. I was a typical missionary, too. I prayed about everything—my meals, my family, which direction to walk, the lessons I taught. As I looked at myself in the mirror in that tiny bathroom, I decided I would do what my companion said. I would pray about cutting my hair. I knelt on the light rug covering the tile floor. I didn't ask Heavenly Father IF I should cut my hair—I just quickly said something like, "Please make my haircut okay." I felt a little sheepish, but I didn't want to know if He thought I should cut my hair.

I pinned half of my hair up, thinking that if I cut the hair underneath and it didn't go so well I could hide the poor job under the uncut hair. I turned around so I could see the back of my head in the mirror. I held the scissors in my right hand and my hair in the other. It took a few snips to orient my hands and brains to move the right way. The moment scissors and my hair met I had a sinking feeling I was going to regret the whole thing. But I had to finish what I started. It wasn't easy to get the scissors through my thick mane. As the strands of hair fell I tried to catch them and put them in the garbage. I finally finished that bottom layer and I didn't want to be alone in that tiny bathroom with the mess that was me anymore. I unpinned the long hair. Would it hide my shame?

I got my answer as I walked out of the bathroom and Sister Newbury asked, "WHAT did you do?!!?"

With my eyes on the floor I slowly lifted my lovely locks to show the short, stubby ones underneath. My companion laughed so hard I thought she was going to roll on the floor. I didn't think one so sick could put forth such energy. "I think I need some help," I said, "so stop laughing!"

The twinkle never left Sister Newbury's eyes as she picked up the scissors and tried to make something presentable out of my mistake.

Yes, it was a mistake. I knew that from the start. From that mistake I've learned that prayer is for everything, even the things I don't want to pray about. Heavenly Father cares about every aspect of my life. I wore a crumby haircut for a few days until I could get professional help. That was the consequence that accompanied my poor choice. Prayer can save me from such consequences and much worse if done correctly.

By Holly B. Robison

# For Choices

I sit on the toilet seat in the cramped motel bathroom with my head in my hands. This should not be happening to me. I don't go to *those* parties. I don't date *those* guys. And before tonight, I thought I didn't have *those* friends.

Considering the mess of people I don't know well enough except to know I shouldn't be partying with them, and the multiple cans of beer outside the safety of the bathroom, it's obvious I'm wrong about the friends thing. *She's not that girl,* I keep telling myself, but the boy with my best friend is that guy.

I stand up. I pound the toilet seat in frustration before sinking to the floor, not caring if the partygoers hear me above the noises outside. This weekend was supposed to be an exciting adventure—two days to cheer on my other friends in their dance competition. The reward of seventeen years of trustworthy behavior.

It's dissolved into a nightmare faster than I could've imagined. Several times I remind myself that Liz*, my former best friend—oh, yeah, definitely former—isn't doing this to me. She's doing this for him. I gag and wish I could yank down the shower curtain, but it's my name on the hotel room. *Absolute nightmare.*

With my head between my knees, I take several deep breaths. I feel stupid for not thinking of the solution earlier. I squeeze my eyes shut and weave my fingers together, my fingernails biting against my skin. Tears leak from the corner of my eyes.

*Heavenly Father, what should I do? What can I do?* I pray silently.

The answer comes like a punch in my gut. *Leave.*

I have no idea where to go. I rip some toilet paper off the roll and mop my face, then splash water on it. Desperately wanting Liz and the others to see me as brave, I wave my hands in front of my face, willing away the redness in my eyes.

I pull open the door. Without a thought for any of my stuff I march out, striding past the two beds crammed with people. I weave through chairs crowded with more people. I ignore the music and the beer. I ignore Liz's plaintive voice asking, "Kara? Kara*, what's wrong?"

Luckily I'm the one with the car. What a blessing, although I would've walked across town rather than stay another minute there. Now that I'm out in the fresh air I wonder what took me so long to get out in the first place. No, I don't go to those parties, not even when they're in a hotel room I saved up for months to pay for.

Once locked up safely in my car I consider my options. I need to call Jan*. She's with the dance team. I don't know if I can stay with them, but she's probably calmer than me at the moment. She'll know what to do.

She answers after two rings. Before she even finishes saying hello, my story tumbles out amid more tears.

"Kara? Hang on just a sec, okay? Everything's going to be just fine, okay? Just fine."

"Okay." I suck in some deep breaths and listen to the murmur of voices on the other end of the line.

Another calming tone replaces Jan's a minute or so later. "Kara? This is Sister Nelson*." Warmth rushes through my limbs. My Young Women's president, Jan's mom. The dance-team parent sponsor. It all seems too much of a coincidence that she's with Jan.

"Hi, Sister Nelson." I hope she hears the gratitude in my voice.

"Can you come over here? You can stay the night with us."

I gulp back a rush of relief. "Yeah. I have my car. I can come."

"Good. See you in ten, Kara."

"Thanks, Sister Nelson."

When I reach the lobby of their hotel, Sister Nelson and Jan envelop me in their arms. I don't think then to thank Heavenly

Father that they're here. Later, when I'm lying between Jan and Brie*, another girl in our ward, I squeeze my eyes shut and cry again—for my blessings.

For my car.

For the strength to walk away from Liz.

For borrowed pajamas and a toothbrush from the gift shop.

For faith.

For friends like Jan.

And even for choices.

*Names have been changed.

By Kara Clark

GOOD
WORKS

Therefore let your light so shine before this people,
that they may see your good works and
glorify your Father who is in heaven.

−3 Nephi 12:16

# Ivy's Cookies

The clank of the metal door and the echo of their footsteps rang in Ivy's and Joanne's ears as they walked down the dingy corridor behind the prison guard toward the "big room." The aroma of Ivy's homemade chocolate-chip cookies wasn't enough to override the stench of ammonia from the recently mopped floor, or the bitterness and anger that hung in the air. Women's Correctional Institute was not the kind of place where seventeen-year-olds go for an outing, but Ivy had a mission.

She didn't know what she was getting into, but she had to try. With trembling fingers, she had dialed the number for an appointment at the prison. Warden Baylor was receptive to Ivy's desire to visit and referred her to Joanne, another teen who had expressed interest.

"How do we do this?" Ivy had asked.

"Who knows? Maybe homemade cookies would break the ice," Joanne suggested.

So they baked their cookies and here they were, bearing gifts to strangers. "I put almonds in these," Ivy rambled nervously as they moved along. "The dough was gummier than usual . . ."

"Don't chatter," the guard snapped. "It gets the prisoners riled."

The harsh words made Ivy jump and her heart pound. She walked the rest of the distance in silence.

"Okay. Here we are," the guard grunted, keys rattling. "You go in. I'll lock the door behind you. Be careful what you say. They have a way of using your words against you. You have fifteen minutes. Holler if you have any trouble." Ivy noted the prisoners' orange jumpsuits and felt overdressed. *Maybe we shouldn't have worn heels,* she thought. *They probably think we're snobs.*

Remembering the guard's admonition, the girls put the cookies on the table next to plastic cups of juice without a word. Some prisoners leaned against the wall; others stood around, watching. Studying. Thinking. Staring. Nobody talked. Ivy smiled at one of the women, and she scowled back. From then on, Ivy avoided eye contact. After five minutes of strained silence, Joanne whispered, "Let's move away from the table. Maybe they'll come over."

As they stepped back, one of the prisoners blurted out, "I'm gettin' a cookie." The others followed and began helping themselves. Soon they heard the rattle of keys. Time was up.

"What a relief to get outta there." Joanne sighed as a gust of fresh air caressed their perspiring faces.

"Yeah," Ivy agreed. "But there's a tug inside me that we're not done. Would you be willing to go back?"

Joanne nodded with a half smile. "How about Thursday after school?"

Week after week they came. And week after week the prisoners ate the cookies, drank the juice, and stood around in silence. Gradually, antagonistic looks were replaced by an occasional smile. Still, Ivy couldn't bring herself to speak—not a word.

Then one Thursday, an evangelist walked in. Her step was sure, her chin was high, and she glowed with the love of God. But she meant business. "I've come to pray with you," she announced. "Let's make a circle."

Ivy was awed by the inmates' compliance. Only a few resisted. The others, although murmuring, inched their way toward the middle of the room and formed a lopsided circle, looking suspiciously at one another.

"Join hands," the evangelist instructed. "It's not gonna hurt ya, and it'll mean more if you do." Slowly they clasped hands, some grasping hard, others barely touching. "Now, bow your heads." Except for the orange outfits, it could have been a church meeting.

"Okay. We're gonna pray," she continued, "and prayer is just like talking, only to God. I want to hear you tell the Lord one thing you're thankful for. Just speak it out. Don't hold back."

Ivy's palms were sweaty. *I can't pray out loud, Lord. I can't even talk to these women. Guess I should set an example, but they probably don't even like me—think I'm better than them because of my clothes.*

The words of an inmate jolted her from her thoughts.

"I'm thankful, God, for Miss Ivy bringing us cookies every week."

Another voice compounded the shock, "God, thanks for bringing a black lady to see us, not just Quakers and Presbyterians."

Ivy's eyes brimmed with tears as she heard, "Thank you, God, for these two ladies givin' their time every week even though we can't do nothin' to pay 'em back."

One by one, every inmate in the circle thanked God for Ivy and Joanne. Then Joanne managed to utter a prayer of gratitude for the prisoners' words. But when it came Ivy's turn, she was too choked up to speak. Her eyes burned in humble remorse over how wrong she'd been about these women. She wished she could blow her nose, but the inmates were squeezing her hands so tightly, she resorted to loud sniffles and an occasional drip.

The following week, Ivy and Joanne returned, bright-eyed, to find the prisoners talkative.

"Why do you bring us cookies every week?" a husky voice inquired from the corner of the room. When Ivy explained, the inmate inched a few steps closer. "Can you get me a Bible?" she asked. Others wanted to know more about the Jesus who inspires teenagers to visit prisoners.

A ministry was born from Ivy's cookies. What started as a silent act of kindness and obedience turned into a weekly Bible study at the prison that eventually grew so big it split into several groups that continue to this day. After Joanne married and moved away, Ivy continued to minister to the inmates alone for years. Eventually, Prison Fellowship picked up the baton.

Ivy is a grandmom now. Her radiance has increased over the years, and she brightens any room she enters. But last Thursday afternoon she indulged herself in a good cry. Curled up on the couch, wrapped in the afghan her daughter had made, she wept. Deep sobs wracked her body as she remembered it had been one year since her daughter died of asthma. She ached over the loss and felt, for the first time, the full weight of her words "The kids can live with me." The baby was asleep in his crib, and the two girls were in school when the doorbell rang.

There stood a young woman, probably seventeen, with a plate of homemade cookies.

"Are you Ivy Jones?" she asked.

"Yes," she answered, dabbing her eyes with a wadded tissue.

"These are for you," the girl said as she handed the cookies to her with a shy, sad smile, turning to leave without another word.

"Thank you," Ivy whispered in a daze. The girl was halfway down the sidewalk when Ivy called out, "But why?"

"My grandmother gave me her Bible before she died last week, and her last words were, 'Find Ivy Jones and take her some homemade cookies.'"

As the girl walked away, a wave of precious memories, uncertainties and younger days flooded Ivy's soul. Swallowing the lump in her throat, she choked back a sob and headed toward the phone. It had been a long time since she'd talked with Joanne.

By Candy Abbot

# Why Don't You Come, Too?

Jennifer sat with her friends around their usual table in the cafeteria, listening to them talk about some youth conference they were going to over spring break. It was being held by their church. Normally, she had as much to say as anyone, but this was something she knew very little about.

Jennifer had been raised an atheist. Her parents did not believe in God or any higher being. Religion was not discussed in her house at all. They celebrated Christmas and Easter, but only the "commercialized" parts like Santa Claus and the Easter Bunny.

But Jennifer had always been curious about religion. She tried to pray on her own once in a while. Occasionally she would attend a church service with a friend, but nothing really impressed her. At times she would ask friends if they believed in God. If they answered yes, Jennifer would pepper them with questions: "What's He like? How do you know He's there? Where does He live? Where does the Bible come from?"

Usually the answer was "I don't know." Eventually, Jennifer stopped asking so many questions.

Then in high school, Jennifer became friends with Roselle, a girl two years older than her. Their friendship quickly deepened, and it seemed that they had known each other forever. Jennifer really looked up to Roselle and had been pulled into Roselle's group of friends.

Now, as everyone else at the table talked about how excited they were for this youth conference and what they were planning to wear, Jennifer felt a little left out. Everybody else in their group belonged to the LDS Church. It was really the only thing she didn't have in common with the others.

Roselle, sitting to her right, suddenly seemed to notice that Jennifer was very quiet.

"Hey, Jennifer," she said, "Why don't you come, too?"

The conversation at the table stopped, and everyone looked over at Jennifer. Then they all started talking at once.

"Yeah, Jennifer, you should come with us."

"You would totally have so much fun."

"It'll be great! You'll love it!"

Jennifer shook her head and held up her hands to stop them.

"I don't think so, guys. I'm not even a member of your church, you know."

"That's okay," Roselle said. "Anybody can come, and you're one of our friends. We can't leave you out. It wouldn't be as much fun without you."

Jennifer came up with other excuses. She had a part-time job, so she couldn't go to the whole conference. She would have to get permission from her parents. She would have to find a way to get there after work. Eventually, her friends convinced her to come to at least part of the youth conference, on the condition that her parents would let her.

At home, she brought up the subject of going to the youth conference and was a little surprised when her parents said it was okay with them. They knew Roselle and some of her other friends and had always thought they were nice girls. Jennifer's mother even agreed to pick her up after her job and drive her to the conference, then come to get her again each evening.

Jennifer did have a lot of fun at the workshops and classes she was able to attend. A lot of what was going on was completely new to her, but Roselle stuck close and helped her feel more comfortable. What impressed Jennifer the most was the testimony meeting at the end of the youth conference. As she watched each person, including Roselle and the rest of her friends, walk to the front of the room and talk about their feelings about the conference and their testimony of Jesus Christ, she had a sudden, very strong feeling that these kids were happy—and a very strong desire to have what they had.

The youth conference was in February. By the end of the school year, Jennifer knew she wanted to join the LDS Church. She talked to her friend's bishop, who told her she would have to take the discussions with the missionaries first. She was finally baptized on July 23.

Looking back, Jennifer remembers, "Of course, I was feeling the Holy Ghost, possibly the first time I had ever felt it and recognized it. I know that my own spirit ABSOLUTELY KNEW what I was feeling, even though I didn't." Jennifer is eternally grateful her friend Roselle did not want her to be left out.

Roselle graduated that spring just before Jennifer was baptized and went on to Ricks College, now BYU–Idaho. The two girls stayed in touch, and Roselle introduced Jennifer to her roommate Brenda, who also became a good friend. During Jennifer's first year at Ricks, she majored in animal science. Brenda's family owned a dry farm and cattle ranch near Ashton, Idaho, and she brought Jennifer home to watch the branding. There, Jennifer met Brenda's older brother, Brodie. The two fell in love and were married in the Idaho Falls Temple. They are now the parents of several children.

By Jennifer Harshbarger, as told to Marta O. Smith

# A Japanese Book

Cami* caught my elbow. "JoLyn, will you help me with something?"

I turned and looked at Cami, whose short brown hair was gelled up in spikes. She'd progressively been cutting it shorter all year. "Yeah."

"Great. Come with me." She pulled me toward the office.

"What are we doing?" I couldn't help the note of skepticism in my voice. Cami was kind of impulsive, the kind of person who didn't get fazed easily. Once she told my father the prophet had counseled parents to get to know their children's friends better, and then invited herself to dinner. Now I wondered what I was getting myself into.

We came to a stop by the brick wall outside the ticket office, where the secretary took payments for concerts, books, and anything else involving money. The office also sold candy bars and other snacks. Maybe Cami needed food but didn't have enough money for anything else. That wouldn't surprise me. Sometimes I felt like I needed to watch out for her.

Cami looked both ways, apparently making sure the other kids in line were too distracted to listen to us. She leaned forward, her green eyes wide. "Okay," she whispered, "I don't want to make a big deal or anything, but I'm kind of nervous about this, so I just want you to come with me. I know you can keep a secret."

"Uh—" I started, wondering if I needed to be worried.

She interrupted. "Do you know Spencer*?"

"Spencer who?"

"You know, the one in our Japanese class." She tugged at the edge of her black shirt.

I tilted my head to one side. I'd never seen her like this. She really might be nervous. I thought back to our Japanese class and remembered a boy named Spencer who sat across the row from us. "Yeah, I know him."

"Good." The line moved forward. She paused again to make sure no one heard. "He doesn't have a Japanese book."

"What?" Of all the things I expected her to say, this was the least likely.

"He couldn't afford one, so I want to buy it, but I don't want him to know it was me. I'm going to pay for it, and then give it to Coach to give to him. I want you to come with me, for moral support, kinda."

It was halfway through the school year. I couldn't believe anyone had managed to go that long in Japanese without the book. I hadn't even noticed. I studied Cami's face. I spent so much time thinking I needed to look out for her, but I'd never seen this side of her. Everything about it caught me off guard.

I gave her a smile. "Okay."

I felt a little weird standing there while she told the secretary Spencer's name and said she wanted to buy his book. She counted out coins to get the total, and I knew it must be her own money.

After leaving a confused secretary, we made our way to Coach's room. Coach taught the Japanese class. As we walked, I couldn't help but be amazed by Cami. This was the sort of thing I read about in stories, heard about in church. I'd never actually seen it happen. For a moment I wondered why I never saw the need, never noticed Spencer trying to learn Japanese without a book. Perhaps I'd been too caught up in my own life to see what Cami saw.

Coach didn't understand at first, but Cami persisted.

"Please just give it to him for me."

Coach seemed to think I was in on it as well. He studied both our faces. I wished I could explain that it was her idea. I was just there for moral support.

"Okay, I'll do it."

Cami sighed. "Great. Let's go, JoLyn."

Outside the classroom, the lunch bell rang.

"Thanks, Jo. I'll see you later." Cami took off.

I watched her go. Maybe she thought she needed me there, but in my heart, I knew she didn't. A shiver of warmth spread through me. She'd let me watch her gift unfold.

I knew I would never forget that lesson. A chance to give might be right in front of me, if I'd only take the time to see.

*Names have been changed.

By JoLyn Brown

# Tender Feet, Tender Mercies

I had just moved to Arizona with a friend on a whim with only a week's worth of clothes and a pair of shoes. We had been at another friend's wedding in Utah earlier in the week and I had come down from Washington State, which is why I had limited luggage. While I was there, my friend talked me into just leaving then and moving down to Arizona, telling me what a fun summer it would be. I was twenty and easily influenced by fun, so I took her up on the offer.

I didn't have much money when I got there, but we had a place stay and I had gas in my old Jeep. We started looking for jobs right away. I had only been there a couple days when one of my shoes broke in half. They were a pair of hiking sandals I'd had for a few years, so I shouldn't have been surprised.

We went to an inexpensive shoe store, and I managed to find some shoes on my small budget. It was a slip-on pair of shoes that covered most of the foot. They were light brown and made of a soft material. I tried on my size and they didn't fit. I was shocked! I'd worn this size for years. My friend told me to just try the next size up. I didn't want to wear the next size up, but I tried them on anyway and they fit perfectly, so I bought them.

That night we went out to a friend's house to play on a rope swing down at the river. When we were walking back my shoes started slipping around, and it was obvious they were too big. I knew it! It was too late to take them back since we had walked through the dirt and a little mud, so I was stuck with them until I got a job and made some money.

The next day we were driving on the main street in town and were stopped at a light. My jeep didn't have a top or doors on it, and an older homeless man came up and asked us for money. At first I thought, *I don't even have money for myself, let alone someone else.* The girls I was with didn't have money, either. As I started telling the man I didn't have any money, I looked at his feet. He wasn't wearing shoes, and he had sores on his feet. While I didn't have money to give him, I told him it looked like he could use some shoes. I handed him one of the shoes I was wearing and asked if he wanted them. He lifted one foot up and brushed off the rocks and dirt that were stuck to the bottom. He slid on the shoe and it was a perfect fit.

I gave him the other one, and he looked me in the eye and said, "God bless you."

"He does, every day," I replied.

We drove off and my friends said, "That was nice," but they wondered what I was going to do for shoes now.

I said, "I'll probably get a job before he will, so I'll just buy new ones later."

Later that day I got a job as a carhop. I borrowed some shoes that didn't fit so well for the interview. For the job they wanted us to wear roller skates, which they provided for us. That was perfect for my no-shoe situation. If fact, they paid us extra if we wore the skates. Also, because we were carhops we got to keep our tips every day, so I didn't have to wait two to four weeks for a paycheck to buy new shoes.

I learned that day that choices aren't always easy, especially when we don't see a solution or what the outcome will be, but that God will bless each of us when we do what we know is right.

By Wendy Singer

# One Friend

The suicide at our high school left everyone asking, "Why?" Could other struggling souls be rescued from a similar heartbreaking end? In the wake of this devastating event, the counselors at Jordan Ridge* had created a plan of action. Each counselor would identify students whom they thought might be "at risk" and interview each student personally.

I attended Jordan Ridge with a student named Jenny*. She was invisible to most students, walking behind other groups with her face to the ground. She lacked the confidence and social skills to interact with others, and she was not considered beautiful by worldly standards. I saw her yearning to fit in and wept silent tears for her. I knew the pain of poor self-esteem and the rejection of peers in my own life. I had since found a sense of belonging with wonderful friends who shared my interests and standards.

It was with this empathetic heart that I began to reach out to Jenny. My efforts were not magnificent—in fact they were very simple—but as President Monson stated in his October 2009 general conference address, "The needs of others are ever present, and each of us can do something to help someone." At first my conversations with Jenny were limited to our choir class, but I would smile and speak to her every day. Soon I was walking with her to our next classes. It didn't take long before she started to confide in me over the phone.

During these conversations I learned a lot about Jenny's difficult life. Her parents divorced when she was young, and her childhood was fraught with abuse. By the time she reached high school, she was living with her grandparents, when her grandmother died unexpectedly. Jenny had no one to lovingly teach her about hygiene or to put arms around her when she was heartbroken. She had only known dysfunctional relationships and had never been taught social skills. Her best efforts in school only yielded mediocre grades. All of her struggles led to others labeling her as awkward, weird, dumb, or annoying. She just wanted to be loved, but it was hard for her to believe she had any worth. She struggled with feelings of deep depression and hopelessness. She wondered if life was even worth living. Though I spent time listening, understanding, giving reassurance, and encouraging her to get help, I never felt my efforts were of any great benefit to her.

Then one day, my mom came to the high school to pick up some scholarship applications from the school counselor. He said he wanted to share something with her. Without naming any names, he told my mother he had spoken with many at-risk students when he came across a girl who told him about her devastating past and her struggle with depression. He asked her if she had any friends. She replied that she had one friend, Katie Smith*. My mom got very emotional at the mention of my name.

He responded, "I know you are proud of your daughter for all of her academic and extracurricular achievements, but above all of these accomplishments, being a friend to this girl is her greatest. You cannot understand what it means to her."

As I have reflected on this experience over the years, my heart is saddened that I did not do more for Jenny. However, I also rejoice that my meager offering was magnified by the Lord and thus made a greater impact in her life than I could ever have imagined. I realize now that good works do not need to be extravagant or pre-planned. They can be as simple as a warm smile, a word of encouragement, a listening ear, an understanding heart, a comforting embrace, or spontaneous laughter. If we open our eyes, we will see the needs of others and opportunities to serve them. When we courageously reach out with a spirit of love, we just might save someone's life.

*Names have been changed.

By Katie Smith

# Independence Day

The cool mountain air blew across my face as I awoke. There was screaming and moaning all around me, and the smell of blood and dirt were on my face.

I remembered a large truck coming towards us as we were descending the mountain highway. Several colleagues and friends and I were returning home after a successful work retreat. Our bus swerved and then rolled and rolled. I was thrown through the windshield and must have been knocked unconscious. I awoke in severe pain and knew something was very wrong. I could not feel or move my legs.

The next thing I remember was awakening in the hospital to the voice of my husband telling me I was alive. I had survived the deadly crash that had taken the lives of nine of my colleagues and friends. He told me it was a miracle I had survived. And another miracle—I was pregnant.

He also told me I would never walk again. I had broken my back in the crash. I had so many feelings and emotions—especially anger— at that moment. I was told I would have to undergo more surgery to stabilize my spine and back. The baby might not survive. I prayed in my heart for the faith I needed to know all would be all right.

Seven years later I am happy, and I have a miracle daughter. The responsibility for my care has fallen upon my husband and family. My husband has cared for me, carried me, and helped me to raise our little girl. Of course, I wish I could be more independent and get around by myself.

We heard about the opportunity to receive a donated wheelchair from The Church of Jesus Christ of Latter-day Saints. I wanted a wheelchair! The day arrived when we could pick it up. We got there early and waited for the doors to open. I wanted to be one of the first in line. My husband carried me into the beautiful building. We were greeted by friendly, smiling, white-haired American missionaries who had come to the Philippines to distribute the wheelchairs. We were given a number and asked to wait our turn.

Groups of people were being questioned about their abilities and their needs for a wheelchair. We were wheeled over to a bench and greeted, and it wasn't long before we were all laughing and talking. An older American couple was overseeing my group, and there was another couple at the other end of the bench.

I was concerned when I was asked if I had or had ever had a pressure sore. The missionaries said if I currently had a sore, it might delay my getting a wheelchair. I was moved to another room and my skin was examined. The American woman was so nice and so easy to talk with about my situation. Everything was fine, and she said I would receive a chair. I was so happy.

The group found the chair that was right for me. It fit, I fit, and I fell in love with it. I was taught how to use and care for my chair. I was so happy that I could now get around by myself. I now could try to get a job and be more independent at home. Many opportunities are now available to me. In just a short time, we had made new friends and were laughing, crying, and hugging the missionaries. They had come from their faraway homes to help me and others from my country receive wheelchairs. Our lives will be changed forever.

By Dalisay Abaya, as told to Roylene Schnebly

# Hit-and-Run Angel

I wandered slowly across the campus at Brigham Young University–Idaho in my Sunday suit and tie, holding my scriptures under my arm. I wasn't really paying attention to where I was going, just following the sidewalk I was staring down at, while the summer sun beat down on my back. I was there attending a youth conference. The highlight of the week, at least for me, was supposed to be the big talent show. There were so many of us there that week that they held tryouts for the available spots in the show. When it was my turn to audition, I sang "Stars" from Les Miserables. And just a few minutes before I started wandering across campus, I'd learned I didn't make the cut.

I was feeling pretty discouraged and a little lost. See, music had always been a really big deal in my life. Heavenly Father gave me a talent for singing, and I worked hard to develop it. I was in the most elite choir at school, and I participated in school and community musical productions. I had played Horton in *Horton Hears a Who,* and Frederick in *Pirates of Penzance.* I even sang in the choir at church. My mom gave singing lessons, and my dad was a high school band teacher. Music practically ran through my veins.

But I wasn't good enough to be chosen for a youth conference talent show. So now I was just wandering aimlessly around campus, feeling sorry for myself. I think Heavenly Father knew I needed a little help right then, so he sent an angel.

I heard the *click, click, click, click* of someone in high heels running on the sidewalk behind me, then felt a *thwap* on the scriptures tucked under my arm. I looked down at my scriptures and saw a yellow sticky note there, as I heard the *click, click, click, click* running away. By the time I looked up, that anonymous young woman had disappeared.

The note she left said, "I think you have a wonderful voice."

I never even saw her face. But that remarkable daughter of God gave me a message of encouragement at a time when I really needed it. I still have that note. I keep it in my scriptures where I can see it all the time, at 1 Nephi 17. That chapter talks about all the ways the people had been blessed, even when they were in the middle of some really hard trials. It reminds me that even when things don't go the way I would like them to and I'm feeling discouraged, God still cares about me enough to send an angel.

By Michael Seare, as told to Marta O. Smith

# Hill of Tears

"Trek." The word alone gave me shivers of terror. I've heard many stories of the hardships the pioneers faced, especially those in the handcart companies.

Mom and I spent a couple of weeks sewing two old-time dresses, matching bonnets, an apron, and pantaloons, plus a satchel to hold our personal belongings.

"The long dresses and the pantaloons will protect your legs, Ashlee, as you walk and walk and walk." Mom smiled.

I groaned at the "walk and walk and walk" part.

The list of things we could take didn't include makeup and hair stuff. My friends were not happy about leaving their "faces" behind, but I didn't really care. It would be nice not to have to worry about all that for a while. Also off the list were cell phones and other electronics.

"This is supposed to be like a real handcart experience," my dad said. "You won't miss them."

Finally, the day arrived. Our leaders drove us to a remote part of northern Arizona. We gathered for prayer and were then divided into families. I had a new ma and pa and thirteen brothers and sisters. Two of my friends were in my family, along with a really cute guy. This was going to be all right after all.

We struggled as we put together our handcarts, then loaded our satchels and gathered around the cart. Some pushed, but most of us pulled a long rope that was tethered to the front corners of the cart. We quickly learned to balance the yoke by pacing ourselves evenly along the rope and making sure we each shared in the load. We laughed and joked and sang a bunch of Primary songs like "Pioneer Children Sang as They Walked" and "The Handcart Song."

I was hot and so tired. After what seemed like forever, we stopped for a drink. The water was in a large can, like an old-fashioned milk jug. It was warm and tasted tinny. All too soon, we rotated around the wagon and began again.

We plodded along all day. I thought we would stop when it got dark, but we didn't. All three handcart companies, with six families in each, pushed on for several more hours. My feet hurt. I had blisters on my heels and my hands. We had long ago stopped loudly and boisterously singing Primary songs. Now we sang hymns, quietly and reverently, to lift our spirits.

Ma stepped in a hole and twisted her ankle. After some rags were used to bind it, she continued to limp along to the side. Around what must have been midnight, we stopped, laid several big tarps under the pine trees, spread out our bed rolls, and fell asleep immediately.

A trumpet blast woke us all too soon, and after eating some bread and fruit, we began walking again. We had great hope because we knew that today we would arrive in Zion. Soon, that hope began to fade. We stood at the base of a huge, rocky hill that seemed as tall as a mountain.

"This is the Hill of Tears," Pa said. "The handcart members often had to persevere through what seemed liked impossible challenges and trials even when they were exhausted."

"Some even died," Ma added quietly.

After a pause to get a drink and a say prayer for strength, we forged on. This time more of us pushed the cart than pulled. The dirt road was full of deep ruts. Those pulling had the job of steering us away from huge rocks. An agonizing two hours later, we crowned the top of the hill and pulled our cart to the side to wait for the other families.

I sat down, holding the stitch in my side with one hand and wiping the sweat from my face with the other. I was in tears. This was hard—very hard. How in the world did those long-ago people do this for days and even months?

I took my shoes off and tenderly placed bandages—one of the few modern things we brought—on my blisters.

I sat quietly looking back down the trail and was stunned. One of my friends and the cute guy had walked halfway back down the hill and were helping another family push their cart. How in the world did they have the strength and energy to do that?

I continued to watch in awe. Soon my tears were no longer for myself, but for the love I witnessed as the rest of my new brothers and sisters, my pa, and even my ma with her twisted ankle joined the people from the other handcart.

I felt ashamed of myself. How could I just sit here? I needed to help, too. I stood up, legs stiff, feet aching, and stepped carefully down the bumpy hill until I found a place pushing a cart next to Ma. Her eyes were wet as she smiled at me. I noticed that each time she stepped on her good foot she pushed the cart. I could see the agony in her face every time her sprained foot touched the ground.

I forced the pain from my blisters and aching muscles out of my mind and pushed as hard as I could, hoping to take some of the load from Ma. I felt so much love for her and for all the others as we pushed and pulled that cart inches at a time up the "Hill of Tears."

I now understand how important it is to sacrifice for others.

The handcart pioneers must have had very powerful testimonies of the Church and gospel of Jesus Christ to suffer like they did and be willing to give everything they had, even their own lives, in order to worship the Lord Jesus Christ.

"Trek." The word no longer brings fear to my heart. Now "trek" means love, faith, and service.

By Cindy R. Williams

INTEGRITY

Till I die I will not remove
mine integrity from me.

—Job 27:5

# To Thine Own Self Be True

Long ago there were seven girls hoeing beets out in a hot field. Six of those girls were eighteen years old, and the other one was twelve. I was the twelve-year-old. The weeds were bad; the hoeing was hard—seventeen rows to the acre. Each time we finished a row it seemed we would never get back to the end of the field again. We knew we weren't making enough money.

The noon sun beat down. We were tired and hot. One girl suggested we stop for a while and go swimming in the canal that ran through the field. Two or three agreed; they were ready to go. One of the girls—I will call her Amy—objected. "We haven't any suits." The other girls talked, argued, coaxed until we had finished our rows and were on the canal bank.

I was not old enough to enter into the discussion. Never, never have I seen so much pressure put on a single person to do that which she knew she should not. I have never forgotten. At first Amy resisted feebly with excuses and protests. As they increased the pressure, her refusals became stronger and firmer. Finally, in answer to their "Why not?" she told them, "I promised myself I would never go swimming naked." Then the other girls really laughed. One of them asked her, "Who's going to know if you break a promise to yourself? Who's going to care?" Amy replied, "I'll know, and if I can't keep a promise I make to myself, how can I keep a promise I make to anyone?"

Years later in a Shakespeare class, I came across that bit of advice old Polonius gave to his son Laertes: "This above all: to thine own self be true, And it must follow, as the night the day, Thou canst not then be false to any man" *(Hamlet,* act 1, scene 3, lines 78–80).

Immediately to my mind flashed a picture of that courageous girl, who said it this way, "If I can't keep a promise I make to myself, how can I keep a promise I make to anyone?"

I've never forgotten the lesson I learned that day in that beet field. It has helped me many, many times. It still does.

By Marjorie South

# The Photo Project

When I was an advertising student in Pasadena, California, we had a combined project with a photography class. We were assigned to art-direct a photo essay showing two disparate groups. Our group chose something like square dancers and surfers. Another group in the class decided to photograph East LA gangsters and Mormons. Everyone laughed at the contrast. I smiled too and thought it would be a visually compelling project. But then the photography teacher started saying disparaging things about members of the LDS Church. He gave examples of photos they should take showing Mormons in a derogatory manner. I wanted to run and hide.

I knew I needed to speak up. I prayed for help. All the students in my department knew I was Mormon. My teacher knew I was Mormon. She looked embarrassed by the photo teacher's comments. She looked at me and I prayed some more. And this great idea came into my mind. I raised my hand and said, "Yes, I really like this idea of shooting the combination of Mormons and gangsters. I am Mormon, and I would love to talk with you more about my church." (The photography teacher went pale.) I said, "It will be a great project. In fact, if you'd like to get fantastic photos, there is a visitor's center behind that large Mormon temple on Santa Monica Boulevard. You can get shots of that temple from the visitor's center side without getting run over by cars. There are people there who will spend all day with you. They will answer your questions, they will let you photograph them, and they might even feed you lunch."

After the class I was bombarded by the group. They wanted the address of the visitor's center. They were so fired up. They all knew someone who knew gangsters they could photograph, but they had been worried about finding Mormons. The end result was a gorgeous photo essay. Little old temple workers in their white suits standing in front of the Los Angeles Temple looking confidently at the viewer. A family that had been sealed together. The photos were stunning. None of them were in the derogatory light the photography teacher had suggested.

During the final critique my teacher asked me to comment on the project. The photography teacher wouldn't look at me (in fact, years later, he still avoided eye contact). I thanked the group for going to the source to represent the Church. They had gone to east LA for the gangster part and participated in a barbecue with some cousin's cousin's gang. The gang photos were authentic and gorgeous.

I thanked the students for showing an authentic portrait of Mormons, rather than a caricature. It was a great opportunity.

"Be strong and of a good courage. Be not afraid, neither be thou dismayed; for the Lord thy God is with thee whithersoever thou goest" (Joshua 1:9).

By Michelle Budge

# Standing Up to Profanity

In the beginning of the school year, we were playing football in gym class. My gym teacher picked the people who knew how to play the best and told them to be team captains. Once the team captains had chosen their teams, I found myself on a team with all boys, except one girl I didn't really know. Our team captain, Alex*, had picked all of his friends to be on his team. As Alex explained the rules, he kept using the Lord's name in vain. Play commenced, and Alex couldn't go sixty seconds without somehow exclaiming Heavenly Father's or Jesus' name in a crude way. I knew I should say something, but I was afraid. I didn't want Alex to be mad at me or feel like I was bossing him around. Anytime someone messed up or his friends would goof around, he would swear and use the Lord's name in an irreverent manner.

Finally, I took a deep breath and marched over to Alex. Even though I was scared, I knew I couldn't just stand there and let him keep swearing and using the Lord's name inappropriately. I also knew Heavenly Father wouldn't want me to let him keep talking like that. "Alex, please stop swearing and using the Lord's name like that."

"Why?" he asked.

"Because He's my Savior. And that language offends me."

"No. I'm not going to stop just for you. I have freedom of speech." He sauntered away without another word. Hurt and puzzled, I walked over to my position on the field. I had done the right thing, so why didn't he listen to me? In the distance, I heard him scream another vile word. I shot him a displeased look.

Throughout gym period, Alex kept swearing and taking the Lord's name in vain, and every time I asked him politely to stop.

I never raised my voice—I just asked him nicely. Our teammates heard our exchanges, and eventually Josh*, one of Alex's friends, said, "Just stop, okay? Just listen to her."

"No," Alex shouted in disgust. I didn't know Josh, nor did I really like him. In fact, I had heard him swear a couple times in the beginning of class too, but I was pleasantly taken aback by what he'd said to Alex. I shot Josh a smile and started to walk over to thank him, but then we were told to get into position to play.

The next day in gym, we played football again in the same teams. Alex continued to swear and take the Lord's name in vain right and left as we faced a new team. I asked him again to please stop. He ignored me. Five minutes later I asked him again, but this time his response was different. "Out of pure respect for you, I will stop. Okay?"

I thanked him, but he didn't even wait for my response before walking away. I smiled to myself and offered a silent prayer of thanks.

I know the Lord blessed me for my persistence. I know He softened the heart of my classmate. I'm grateful for a loving Heavenly Father who watches over me. I'm glad I was able to have the courage and patience it took to influence my peer for good.

*Names have been changed.

By Whitney Churchill

# Don't You Know Who He Is?

During my last year at Ricks College, I was taking a New Testament class, studying the life and teachings of Jesus Christ as found in the books of Matthew, Mark, Luke, and John. Along with the scriptures, there was a rather lengthy student manual that went with the course, containing doctrinal commentary and insights into the people and culture during the time of Christ. I really enjoyed listening to the lectures in class. I had always liked my religion classes and soaked up everything I heard.

However, I was not very diligent with the reading assignments. I had homework from my other classes, my work on the student newspaper, and my social life, which all seemed to take priority over actually studying for my religion class. I didn't think it would be a problem, since I already knew all that stuff anyway.

Near the end of the semester, our teacher informed us that a large part of our final grade would be determined by how much of the reading we had finished. We would be asked to report this on our final exam, and we were on our honor. By my calculations, my grade on the reading portion would hover between an F and a D. That brought me up short.

I had three options. I could be dishonest and say that I had done all the reading so that I could get an A in the class. That wasn't even a real consideration, because I had always been taught by my parents to be honest. Just the thought of cheating gave me stomach pains.

I could honestly report how much of the reading I had done and fail the class. That seemed nearly as bad as the first option. I had been a member of the LDS Church all my life. I had always been the smart kid in Sunday School who knew the answers to the teacher's questions. I was attending a Church-owned college. There was no way I was going to flunk a religion class.

This left the third option: Finishing all the reading assignments, most of a semester's worth, in just over a week. I decided I would spend every spare minute reading. I might not get an A, but I was determined not to fail. I carried my scriptures and student manual with me everywhere. I read on my way to and from classes. I read as I sat waiting for other classes to start. Sometimes, I even read during my other classes, though I tried to be very discreet about it. I read while I cooked my meals and while I ate and while I did my laundry. I spent the entire day that Sunday, except for my time driving to and from church, reading from the New Testament.

The manual had divided up the four Gospels into reading blocks that grouped the events of Christ's life in chronological order. Instead of reading each Gospel straight through, the idea was to be able to read what each of the apostles had recorded about a specific event, and then read the commentary on that event. It meant a lot of flipping pages back and forth, but it also afforded an immersion into the life and teachings of Christ, more or less in order.

It all seemed more vivid and interesting to me than ever before. But as I read the accounts of the last week of the Savior's life, I began to dread what I knew was coming. I read of the triumphal entry, the last supper, and Christ's great intercession in the Garden of Gethsemane. I read of His betrayal and how He was taken first before the Sanhedrin, then to Pilot, to Herod, and back to Pilot. I read how a mob demanded He be crucified, and how they requested the release of a murderer in His stead.

Finally one gray, overcast afternoon, I sat in the utility room of my apartment, reading as I washed my laundry. The little room was lit by a single bulb hanging from the ceiling. Pilot washed his hands. The soldiers took Jesus away and scourged Him.

Then I read Matthew 27:30. "And they spit upon him, and took the reed, and smote him on the head." Nearly in tears, I wanted to yell at them, "How can you do that to Him? Don't you know who He is?"

Suddenly it was as though the light in the room changed, became brighter. My mind was literally enlightened. The Roman soldiers may not have known who He was, but I did. I KNEW WHO HE WAS! This was my Savior, Jesus Christ, I was reading about. In that moment, He became more real to me than He had ever been before, as real as any of my friends or the classmates I saw every day. He literally lived on this earth, died for my sins, and was resurrected.

I don't remember what grade I got on the final of my New Testament class, but I passed. It was the best class I've ever taken.

By Marta O. Smith

# The Dance Decision

I came home from volleyball practice with a splitting headache. I had never had a migraine, but this sure felt like one. My head was pounding behind my eyes, I felt nauseated, and the slightest sound or light caused my head to spin. I decided to take some Tylenol, lie down in my dark bedroom, and try to sleep it off. I would only get one hour of shut-eye before I had to leave to attend the ballroom dance competition at BYU that night and do a write-up for my Latin dance class at UVSC. I devised my plan carefully to make every minute count. I changed into clean clothes so I would be ready to go, set my alarm, and fell half-conscious on my bed.

I was famous for pushing myself to the limit. In high school, I was a 4.0 student and graduated at the top of my class. I also participated in volleyball, madrigals, and drama. My schedule was no less rigorous now that I was in college. I took every honors class available, played collegiate volleyball, and maintained my 4.0 GPA, knowing I needed good grades to maintain my presidential academic and athletic scholarships.

I was suddenly awakened from my state of unconsciousness only to have the ugly numbers of the clock glaring back at me. It was 9:00 PM! Half dazed, half in shock, I shot straight up in bed. I had missed the competition. My mind started racing through possible solutions. I grabbed the phone and quickly dialed a friend's number.

"Hello," he answered.

I struggled to speak through my tears. "Hey, Jeff, I missed the competition. I came home from practice with a horrible headache and lay down to rest, but I overslept my alarm. Did you go?"

"Yeah, I went. Look, don't even worry about it. It will be fine.

I have a couple extra programs. You can have one to hand in, and I will help you with the write-up. It's not like you missed it on purpose. It wasn't your fault. Besides, I am doing the same thing for another classmate."

My mind was reeling. The only time I had ever cheated was on a spelling test at age six. Luckily, first graders are not very good at cheating, and my favorite teacher had caught me. When I got the test back with a big red "0" on it and a note from Miss Carter, I was devastated and ashamed. I apologized to her profusely and vowed to never cheat again.

That was before the age of accountability, and there was a lot less on the line. There was a lot more to lose now—my perfect 4.0, my valuable scholarship, and my integrity. All for what, a stinking elective dance class? It wasn't fair and it wasn't my fault. Heavenly Father would understand, right? None of my rationalizations sounded right even in my desperation. I knew integrity was the most precious thing on that list, and it was not something I was willing to sacrifice. After calling my mom, sobbing as I explained my dilemma, I had no doubt what I needed to do.

I walked into class early the next day, my heart pounding, pulse racing, palms sweating. I wanted to catch the teacher early before all the other students arrived. "Um, Mr. A., can I talk to you for a minute?" I said.

"Sure, Michelle, what can I do for you?" he replied.

I explained the whole situation and apologized for missing the dance performance. I realized that the write-up was a large part of the grade and that without it I could not get higher than a "B" in the class. Was there anything I could do to make up the extra points? He stared at me in amazement for just a moment, and then the words came.

"You didn't know you could go to another dance performance and do a write-up?" he asked incredulously.

"No, I had no idea," I responded sheepishly.

"In fact there's one coming up next week," he added.

I wrote down the date, location, and time, then thanked him for his understanding and for the information.

He stopped me as I turned to get ready for class. "I have to commend you for your honesty, Michelle. You have no idea how many students skip the performance, get programs from classmates, and then fake the write-up. It's really refreshing to know there are students like you."

I danced on air that day. I went on to graduate with a 4.0, a departmental award, and an honor's degree, but none of these accomplishments would have meant anything if I had compromised my values for a grade. The greatest honor came from the peace I felt knowing I had done what was right and pleasing to my Father in Heaven. I felt to exclaim with Job, "God forbid that I should justify you: till I die I will not remove mine integrity from me" (Job 27:5).

By Michelle Bennett Diehl

# A Star-Spangled Heart

My twin sister Jessica and I were at our locker getting our books for our first class. She was going to Spanish 2, and I was going to AP European History. We were singing the song "Journey to the Past" from the movie *Anastasia,* specifically the beginning.

*Heart don't fail me now*
*Courage don't desert me*
*Don't turn back now that we're here.*
*People always say*
*Life is full of choices*
*No one ever mentions fear.*

As we parted ways, I continued to hum this song on my way to class. It felt like the song was permanently stuck in my head. After I entered the classroom, I quietly sat in my seat in the front row, in front of the teacher's desk. I placed my copy of *Pride and Prejudice* by Jane Austen on my desk, amazed I was halfway finished with it.

My thoughts turned to what the teacher had said the day before. He gave us a reason why he doesn't stand for the pledge of allegiance. I thought his reason was silly, and I could tell that his opinion of the pledge had become the opinion of some of the other students. It really showed because standing for the pledge had been a struggle all year long. Only two or three students would stand, including me.

As I heard the announcement to stand for the pledge, I quickly stood up, wondering who would stand up today. To my surprise I was the only one. Usually, another girl would stand every day, but she explained later that she felt sick and had homework to finish. I would have stood by myself but I could not find the flag, for it was not in its normal place.

"Journey to the Past" started playing over and over in my head: "Heart don't fail me now . . . no one ever mentions fear." The idea went through my head that they were playing a joke on me and hiding the flag. I could feel the tears starting to build up, and to make it worse I heard some people snickering. (I later figured out that they were not snickering at me, but it sure felt like it at that moment.)

I said quietly, "Where's the flag?" but no one said anything. Then I turned to my teacher and with all the breath that was left in me, I whispered, "Where's the flag?" He put his head down and snickered also. I didn't know what to do. The second line of the song came back to me—"Courage don't desert me." But I had no more courage left. It had all deserted me as I sat down with tears bursting out of my red, swollen eyes.

I don't have the talent of talking out loud about something that has hurt me. Instead, I write about it. So with that in mind, I took the yellow sticky note in front of me and started to write all that I was feeling. It started with reasons why I stand for the pledge and how it is very dear to my heart. Then I wrote of the class and how disappointed I was with all of them, how they have no respect for our country. Then I wrote that I wished my teacher had not seated me in the front row, as well as a few other things I was feeling.

As the bell rang and everyone left the classroom, I found myself alone in the room with my teacher. He asked about the pledge and how it meant something to me, and all I could do was nod my head, because all those tears started to build up again. He was very sweet and asked what we should do about it. When I tried to reply, my tears ran down my cheeks and I burst out in a sob.

I remembered reading in *Pride and Prejudice,* "Mary wished to say something very sensible, but knew not how."

I remembered my thoughts I had written on the yellow sticky note and suddenly had an idea to give it to him. I said through my sobs, "This is for you." Then I handed him the note and ran out of the room.

My parents learned of what happened. Because of their concern, there was an investigation and some of the students in the class were interviewed about what happened that day. Many disagreed with me on what happened, and that made me feel like maybe I was just overreacting. But my mother reminded me to think of how the class and teacher made me feel. It was not something I made up, as some people believed. It really happened, and no one could tell me differently.

Another quote from *Pride and Prejudice* helped me with this. "The more I see of the world, the more am I dissatisfied with it; and every day confirms my belief of the inconsistency of all human characters, and of the little dependence that can be placed on the appearance of merit or sense."

I was in desperate need of comfort and for someone to believe me. There were two girls in my class who agreed with me, and it meant so much. I finally felt like I was doing the right thing. My sister helped me the most. She wrote me a sweet note one day.

*My dearest twin sister,*

*I found the perfect scripture to go along with your situation. It is D&C 68:6. "Wherefore, be of good cheer and do not fear, for the Lord is with you, and will stand by you." So if you say the pledge today, keep this scripture in your mind. Know that Jesus Christ is probably standing (in spirit) next to you, with his hand over his heart. If he was really there I could just imagine how proud he would be of your courage! His eyes would probably sparkle as he watches you stand up when no one else does. I think he'd cry! You are so STRONG and you have so much COURAGE! Show them what's what! Stand tall and smile. You are AWESOME!*

*Your twin sister,*
*Jessica*

From this experience, I have learned to stand up for what I believe. I learned that even if others aren't doing what's right, I don't have to follow them. I should always do what is right and turn to my Heavenly Father when I am in need of comfort or guidance. I now have a deeper understanding of the pledge of allegiance, and I love our country even more than I did before.

By Beth Beach

VIRTUE

Who can find a virtuous woman?
for her price is far above rubies.

—Proverbs 31:10

# no Regrets

I did not expect the letter. Years had passed since I had seen or talked with Patricia. I was a young wife and mother living twenty-five miles away from the high school we had graduated from together in 1978. It all seemed a lifetime away, until I opened the letter. I hadn't thought about my tenth-grade sociology class in years, but the letter brought it instantly back into focus.

The class had gotten into a discussion about the supposed merits of sexual relations before marriage. Mr. Frace, our teacher, served as a silent moderator, pointing to whomever felt they had something to say, then listening with the rest of us. I had already gotten plenty of grief for my commitment to virtue and my views on dating and chastity—I had no intention of participating in the debate. However, as the conversation evolved I felt I could no longer remain silent. Most of the young men in the room were proponents of having sexual experience prior to marriage, though they all wanted to marry chaste girls. It was their eschewed expectations that forced me to speak.

"I have a question. Why the double standard? Do you really think such a girl would want to marry you?"

*Whoosh!* Every eye in the room turned on me. Mr. Frace raised his eyebrows.

"Do you plan to be a virgin on your wedding night?" he asked me?

"Yes, sir, I do."

"And what are your expectations in regards to your future fiancé's virginity?"

"Well, it seems appropriate to expect the same from him. See, I view it as a God-given gift that we should open together."

There was a deafening moment of silence, and then I was faced with an onslaught of angry words from the rest of the class.

The comments continued for a moment with no one backing up my position, until Mr. Frace stood up, walked from behind his desk, and said, "Stop." He said it calmly, almost in a whisper. "I have a confession to make."

Mouths shut, all eyes turned his direction.

"I'm a virgin. My fiancée is, too. We chose to save the gift for each other. We're getting married over spring break. It's a nice place to be—no regrets."

The bell rang, and suddenly the room was empty. I slid out of the door into the busy hall. Mr. Frace followed me. He reached out and touched my arm.

"Thanks. Your words gave me the courage to stop hiding behind the assumptions."

———

Patricia's letter reminded me of that day and her reactions to my words. She had always thought I was naive and teased me mercilessly over the subject. Yet now, her letter expressed a completely different opinion. With the discovery of AIDS and other such diseases, she had become more and more aware of the risks her lifestyle had exposed her to. She shared her fears for her future, then stunned me with her acknowledgement that I had been right all along. My moral standards, my commitment to virtue, had placed me safely in a place where I would never face the fears she was facing. She was right. It was a nice place to be. I had no regrets.

By Teresa B. Clark

# A Shining Light in a Darkened Theater

One certain evening, my husband invited me to see a play with him at the theater in town. It was a group from New York City who was touring the nation, and one of the stops was in our little town of Idaho Falls, Idaho. It was quite a to-do, and everybody who attended was dressed up very formally. Everyone seemed to be buzzing with the excitement of sophistication, and even my husband and I felt a bit fancier than our regular old selves.

After we found our seats and settled in, the lights dimmed and the play began. All eyes fixed toward the front with anticipation. As the play went on, our cheerful spirits soon began to change. The dialogue was filled with inappropriate language and vulgarity, and we became completely uncomfortable.

I looked around, expecting to see the rest of the audience becoming uncomfortable as well. But to my disappointment, nearly everyone seemed perfectly content to listen. I was disappointed that so many were okay with the filth. Just then, a little light of a voice came from behind me.

"Why are we still here?" she said. "Let's go. I am going to leave."

I peeked over my shoulder and caught a quick sight of a young girl around thirteen attending the play with her parents. Her conviction impressed me as she became the shining example of virtue in that darkened theater. She didn't want any part of that type of "sophistication" and was willing to tell her parents that they needed to leave.

My husband and I didn't stay, either, and we left right behind the small family, turning the heads of some surprised patrons. I have never forgotten this girl's high standards or how she bravely spoke out in the midst of a sea of adults. She had the courage to do what was right, and she was a representation of our many virtuous young women.

By Kirsten Hinton

# From Immodest to modest

I've always loved fashion. Growing up I didn't always dress modestly. I didn't really understand the importance of it. But showing more skin never helped me in any way. Actually, it really hurt me. I would only get asked out by junk guys, not the type of guy I was looking for. Later I realized the kind of guy I was looking for would be looking for someone who looked good and dressed cute while still keeping it modest. Showing more skin also hurt me spiritually, because the Spirit would leave whenever I chose to disobey this seemingly small commandment, leaving me open to more destructive influences without its protection. In fact, I can trace back all of my problems and mistakes to the breaking of "small" commandments such as modesty and media standards.

So I made some wrong choices, but then I wised up. I worked hard to be temple worthy and once I did, I met a perfect, awesome guy who married me in the temple.

I had been doing some modeling here and there since I was a young teen. After I got married, my modeling agent called to ask if I'd be interested in being in a fashion show the next weekend. I said sure, and she scheduled me for a fitting. If you're not familiar with the term, a fitting is where you meet with the show coordinators to pick out what you are going to wear and make sure it fits.

As I drove to the fitting I started to get nervous because I wear temple garments now and I wondered what I would say if they wanted me to wear something that didn't comply with my standards. I was hoping I wouldn't have to face that, but in the back of my mind I knew I would.

The fashion show was for the designer Betsey Johnson. When I got to the fitting I didn't see anything in view that I could wear without breaking my standards. The coordinators greeted me and quickly escorted me to a dressing room while they analyzed my body shape and asked what size I wore. They began picking clothes for me. I timidly said, "I'd prefer to wear whatever you have that shows the least skin." They seemed confused but they complied and brought me the most modest clothes they had, all the while reassuring me that I was beautiful and shouldn't be ashamed of showing my body. I looked at these offerings—the least revealing clothing they had— and knew I would have to take my off garments to wear them. I quickly removed my garments and put on the clothing, showing each outfit to the coordinators. Three outfits were decided on and then we were finished. I left feeling awful.

As I drove home I thought about it. The purpose of this fashion show was to persuade people that these clothes looked good and that they were cool. I thought about my struggles with modesty. Growing up I always felt like I had to choose between being modest and looking good. I often abandoned modesty for immodest fashions because I let what I saw in magazines and in other media determine my own idea of what looked good. Why would I want to participate in saying to the world, "This is what looks good—you should wear this," when I actually believe the opposite? I would be participating in the massive lie that deceives so many people just as it had deceived me.

That night I called the fashion-show coordinators and told them I wouldn't be in the show. The girl I talked to asked me why, and I told her it was for religious reasons. She was really respectful toward me and said that she hoped they hadn't offended me or made me uncomfortable.

When my husband overheard me on the phone saying I wouldn't do the show, I heard him say a huge "YESSS!" like guys do when their team wins the Superbowl. And after I got off the phone he told me, "I knew you would do the right thing." I felt a huge wave of peace come over me, and I was happy about my decision.

Because I had chosen the right thing, the Spirit was with me and gave me the idea for jennmagazine.com. I started working on it right away.

By Jennifer Loch

# Orange Juice

One Sunday afternoon, we were just finishing our family dinner when somehow the conversation turned to popular movies. One of my daughters mentioned a very popular movie that had one of those objectionable scenes in it.

She said something like this, "Dad, what's so wrong with that movie? I'd really like to see it. We can always fast-forward that two-minute part."

She knew about the bad part in the movie. She knew it was wrong, but the rest of the movie had captured her imagination, and she wanted to see it.

Instead of arguing with my daughter, I remembered something a friend of mine had done in a class. Sitting on the table was a pitcher of orange juice with just one cup left in the bottom. I poured the last cup, held it up, and asked her if she wanted it. My children love O.J., and of course she wanted it.

"Okay then," I said, "follow me."

With most of my children curiously following, I took the glass of orange juice and walked into the bathroom. I reached into the toilet with another cup and dipped out some toilet water. Ever so carefully, I poured just one tiny drop of toilet water into the orange juice.

I held it out to her. "Here you go," I said.

She screamed and ran out of the bathroom.

"But honey," I said as I held it out to her, "it's only one little drop."

"I don't care!" she yelled. "It's yucky!"

You know, I could not get her to come within ten feet of that glass of orange juice. I finally had to pour it out.

Since that time, I have not had a single argument with any of my children about which movies they should be watching. I hope I never have to.

The prophet Isaiah said, "Be ye clean, that bear the vessels of the Lord" (Isaiah 52:11). To my way of thinking, it is time! For the covenant people, it is time!

By Glenn Rawson

# About the Editors

## MARILYN O. DIEHL

Marilyn O. Diehl taught school at North Davis Junior High in Clearfield, Utah, and the Girl's Rehabilitation Facility for San Diego County, in Santee, California, where she was head of the school's business department for four years and also head teacher at the school for one year. Marilyn has written over one hundred human-interest and religion articles for newspapers in Quartzsite and Parker, Arizona, and Blythe, California. She is currently a guest columnist for the opinion page of *The Post Register* in Idaho Falls, Idaho.

## MARTA O. SMITH

Marta O. Smith has been writing since she discovered the alphabet. She was a reporter and co-editor of her high school newspaper, then a columnist and copyeditor at the Ricks College Scroll. Marta currently blogs at The Last Word (www.martasmith.blogspot.com) and Of Good Report (thingsofgoodreport.blogspot.com). She has won several writing contests and is currently writing a novel.

Marilyn and Marta would like to hear from you. You can contact them at valuesstories@gmail.com.

# Permissions

Abbott, Candace F. , "Ivy's Cookies," *Chicken Soup for the Prisoner's Soul,* compiled by Jack Canfield, Mark Victor Hansen, Tom Lagana (Deerfield Beach, FL: Health Communications, 2000), 102–6. Used by permission.

Budge, Michelle, "The Photo Project," accessed Jan. 10, 2010, from miamaidsrock.blogspot.com. Used by permission.

Clark, Teresa B., "Priceless," adapted from "The Power of Story," accessed Feb. 19, 2009, from Teresaclark.blogspot.com. Used by permission.

Churchill, Whitney, "Be Still and Know That I Am God," accessed Jan. 10, 2012, from Mormon-teen.blogspot.com. Used by permission.

Churchill, Whitney, "Standing Up to Profanity," accessed Aug. 24, 2011, from Mormon-teen.blogspot.com. Used by permission.

Farrell, Heather, "You Already Know," accessed July 10, 2011, from Womeninthescriptures.blogspot.com. Used by permission.

Loch, Jennifer, "From Immodest to Modest," *Fashion Without Compromise— Modest Fashion,* from www.jenmagazine.com. Used by permission.

Rawson, Glenn, "Kassie and the Soap," from *In the Midst of Thee,* Volume II, by Glenn Gawson (Blackfoot, ID: Harmony River, 2009), 132. Used by permission.

Rawson, Glenn, "Orange Juice," from *In the Midst of Thee,* Volume I, by Glenn Rawson (Blackfoot, ID: Harmony River, 2009), 40. Used by permission.

Scoresby, Rose, Ruth Haderlie, and Bertha Christensen, "The Special Flour Barrel," from the family history of Senie Dorthea Nielsen, adapted by Marilyn O. Diehl. Used by permission of Ivy Scoresby Smith, a great-granddaughter of Senie.

Scoresby, Rose, "A True Pioneer Incident," in *Poems of Laughing Living Loving,* by Rose and Austin Scoresby, printed by their family (see pp. 112–13). Adapted by Marilyn O. Diehl as "Left Behind." Used by permission of Ivy Scoresby Smith, a great-granddaughter of Emma.

Tagawa, Linda, "The Lei," in *Chicken Soup from the Soul of Hawai'i,* compiled

—

—